MRS HARVEY'S SISTER~IN~LAW

and other tasty dishes

MARGARET DUNN

MRS HARVEY'S SISTER~IN~LAW

and other tasty dishes

MURDOCH BOOKS

CONTENTS

PART THREE
meat and right

92

Steak and pickled walnuts, Cousin Daisy's Cornish pie, Dunn's famous hot pot, My father's hot pot, Aunt Nellie's veal pie, Short crust, The Contessa's beef burgundy, Hungarian veal, Veal Veronique, Aberdeen sausage, Marjory's grandma's roll, Sheep's head pie, Pressed meat, Mother's savoury steak, Vienna steak, "My" meat loaf, Mrs Gee's sausage casserole, Steak and kidney pudding, Spare ribs, Devilled meat, Dick's curry, Else's pork chops, Huguette's pork fillet, Aunt's rabbit pie, Mother's jellied rabbit, Audrey's rabbit goose, Mother's way with chicken, Ginger chicken, Bishop's chicken.

PART FOUR
eggs, cheese and salad

126

Phil's omelette, Sandwich soufflé, Crabmeat soufflé, Reg's quiche Lorraine, Bishop's delight, Madame Bossard's fondue, Val's pasticcio, Basil's macaroni cheese, Macaroni and mushrooms, FOUR SALADS: Bill's Caesar salad, Norma's rice and tuna salad, Tabooli, "My" potato salad, "My" salad dressing.

PART FIVE
afters

≈ 146 ≈

Mother's roly poly, Auntie Chick's lemon pie, Baked thatch pudding, Mother's lemon pudding, Delicious pudding, Mother's apple charlotte, Luise's apples in sauce, Apple crunch, Our Helen's apple pie, Tarte aux pommes, Baked fruit pudding, Fanny's rhubarb souffle, Boiled steamed apple pudding, Father's apple pudding, Urney pudding, Sago plum pudding, Bridie's plum pudding, Suet pudding, Annie's spotted dick, Mrs Bowden's steam pudding, Orange pudding, Golden dumplings, COLD: Paradise pudding, Angel food, Flummery, Mrs Harvey's sister-in-law, Ardmore pudding, Caramel custard, Polka pudding, Floating island, Ruby's lemon sago, Tasmanian semolina pudding, Egg pudding, Crêt Bérard caramel apples, Gooseberry fool, Summer pudding, Marjorie's mocha cream, Sophie's apricot cream, Mother's lemon butter, Ruby's orange filling, Bushwhacker's tart, Chess pie with marrons, Butter tarts, PANCAKES AND FRITTERS: Apple fritters, Pancakes, Mr Virgin's fritters, CAKES: Hazelnut cake, Pavlova cake, Granny Vaughan's pound cake, Mrs Gatwood's plain cake, Emma's sandwich, Mock cream, Mrs Weston's chocolate cake, Walnut and ginger cake, Pearl's brown walnut cake, Lyle's rum and walnut cake, Mildura tea cake, Daisy cake, Banana cake, Reg's Dundee cake, Never fail cake, Bob's cake, My sister's love cake, Mrs Shew's orange cake, Betty's blow-away sponge, THE COOKIE JAR: Pearl's Tasmanian rocks, Nutties, Mrs Shew's walnut biscuits, Chinese chews, Winsome's biscuits, Caramel biscuits, Mrs Brett's peanut biscuits, Hidden dates, Mrs Oswald's cornflake cookies, Rice bubble biscuits, Ginger creams, Golden crunches, Burnt butter biscuits, Yo-Yo biscuits, Mrs Longbottom's shortbread, Bailey biscuits, Hedgehogs, Ginger and apricot slice.

PART SIX
other things to do
❧ 232 ❧

Mrs Jones' strawberry jam, Mrs Dark's fig jam, Aunt Ethel's fig preserve, Mock ginger, Three-day marmalade, Mildura marmalade, Citron preserve, Preserved cumquats, Cauliflower pickle, Tomato relish, Tomato sauce for immediate use, Peach chutney, Pickled walnuts, Tutti frutti, Orange drink, Helen's barley drink, Mrs French's raisin loaf, treacle loaf, Pufftaloons, Pocket book rolls, Self-raising flour.

PART SEVEN
high days and holidays
❧ 254 ❧

Frances' chocolate birthday cake, Kate's wedding cake, Stephen's Shrove Tuesday pancakes, Jock's spinach pancakes, Simnel cake, Easter bonnet pudding, "My" plum torte, Mère Royaume soup, Mrs Dunn's instant vin chaud, Thanksgiving pumpkin pie.

PART EIGHT
and oh, those Christmases!
❧ 276 ❧

That marvellous turkey stuffing, Greek turkey stuffing, "My" Christmas cake, Mrs Hart's Christmas cake, "My" Christmas pudding, Ruth's mincemeat, THE CHRISTMAS COOKIE TRAY: Chocolate walnut balls, Luise's almond crescents, Butter balls, White Christmas, Mrs Turner's old English mincemeat, Joy's currant pie, Old favourite Christmas sauce.

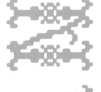

INTRODUCTION

WHEN I FIRST BEGAN PUTTING THESE
RECIPES IN BOOK FORM, OVER THIRTY
YEARS AGO, I DID SO AS A MOTHERLY
PRESENT FOR MY DAUGHTERS, BUT THAT
WAS A LONG TIME AGO AND THINGS
HAVE CHANGED. IT IS STILL A MOTHERLY
PRESENT BUT I MUST NOW OFFER IT TO
MY CHILDREN AND GRANDCHILDREN.
SOME OF THEM LIVE ON THE OTHER SIDE
OF THE WORLD AND I SEE LITTLE OF
THEM. BUT THEY ALL COOK.

SO I OFFER THEM THIS COLLECTION AS I
ONCE DID TO THEIR MOTHERS.

♥ ♥

 *My dear children and grandchildren,*

It may come as a shock to you after all you've been led to believe, but I am not the world's best cook. I am, however, probably among the most enthusiastic.

I feel very strongly about it. For instance, I am convinced we'd have a better world, and better citizens in it, if we built larger kitchens instead of smaller and smaller ones. I know baseball enthusiasts suffer from the same kind of illusion, and just look how the English went around teaching everyone cricket! Me, I'd have put them all into the kitchen.

Sometimes it seems to me that most of my childhood was spent in kitchens. I learned to cook early, not because I particularly wanted to – at least not in the beginning – but simply because I spent so much time among people who did. Cooking was so much part of my life, and the big sunny kitchen the very heart of the home. I suppose it is the advancing years which make me say "the big sunny kitchen", for as

♥ ♥

♥ ♥

we get older I know we are apt to remember our childhood as one long summer. And of course it wasn't. Once in New York I heard Dione Lucas (really the best cook I've ever known) respond to a question about what she had done one dreary, wet Sunday by saying, "I cooked. What else was there to do?" And my mind went skimming back to long wet Sundays when we looked at each other in desperation and said, "Let's make toffee" or "What about hot scones for tea?" Cooking something was The Answer. Winter or summer, the kitchen was the centre of things for us.

And this is the way it should be. There was a real warmth and feeling to it then. A feeling that doesn't grow out of tiny, one-person-at-a-time-sized kitchens, or frozen foods, or labour-saving devices, or instant anythings – convenient as they all may be. A kitchen should be large, warm, embracing and friendly, with a table and chairs so you can sit while chopping or peeling or simply having a cup of tea. It makes my soul curl to hear it referred to as a "food preparation area". Kitchen is a good word, with a heart and a personality of its own.

The recipes I grew up with had personality too. They were not always very clear or logical, but I am not convinced that clarity and logic are always the best ingredients anyway. Imagination is often better, and many of my mother's recipes certainly called for it. Things were

♥ ♥

❤ ❤

not always measured by level spoons or level cup measures. They were much more apt to call for "a pinch" of this or "enough" of that. There was always that "nut" of butter that you put in, without any real knowledge as to whether it meant a peanut or a coconut. There was a certain excitement about all this that the modern, meticulous cookbook misses out on altogether. It involved a good deal of tasting as you went along, and a good deal of serious contemplation of the batter to see if it really was "just a little thicker than good cream". There was a feeling of experimentation, and somehow the same old recipe wasn't always guaranteed to turn out the same old way every single time.

In my childhood kitchen, there was a large blue cup without a handle that was used as a measure when the recipe stated a "breakfast cup", and if it said a "small cup", you measured just up to the broad gold band inside the rim. But there were always those recipes that said a "tea cup", and people drink tea out of all kinds of cups. I was never too sure of that one. As for the gill and the wine glass I've never sorted that out to this day. I was taught that a gill was a wine glass (though whether sherry or champagne no one ever said) and now I have a measuring cup which says, firmly, that it is half a cup. This may be so, but it is not what I was led to believe, and I can quote at least one recipe to show that it isn't always what other people believe

❤ ❤

*My first husband, Robert Paine, and me just before
the war, when we were first engaged.*

either. I still feel that when a recipe says a gill, that's the moment when, rather than trustfully tipping in half a cup, one starts adding little by little, stopping when it feels, tastes or seems right.

It was because of all this vagueness in the recipes that one learned to tell by taste, by consistency, by feel, by look – almost by instinct – how things were going. Sometimes, even with the best recipe in the world, the clearest and the most accurate, this is still the best way of judging.

Recipes in my mother's kitchen all had their own personality because they mostly came from people rather than books. If Mrs Weston gave my mother a recipe for chocolate cake, which she did, it was immediately written in the book as "Mrs Weston's Cake", and usually referred to simply as "Mrs Weston". "Why don't you bake Mrs Weston for the school fête?" my mother would say. Once when I was staying in Sydney and decided to do some cooking, I wired my mother saying, "Will phone tonight, want Mrs Weston". The telegram somehow arrived in the middle of the night, which in wartime is frightening, and threw the entire household into a state of panic. No one could imagine what possible emergency would necessitate my wanting to speak to the rector's wife, or why, if I did need her so badly, I hadn't simply phoned the rectory.

Even printed recipes frequently had names attached; they were personal things from some definite person's kitchen. I don't think my mother quite trusted recipes which didn't have a name to them, and I myself have a slightly uneasy suspicion that some of the more scientifically exact ones that never fail or vary, just might have been whipped up by a computer.

Of course, there was a good deal of suspicion about in those days too. I have cake recipes which say you must bake them in a square tin, or sauces that must be stirred with a silver spoon. I know very well that a round tin and a wooden spoon work just as well, but I never really feel comfortable about using them. I was taught that there was a time of the month no lady attempted a sponge cake because it wouldn't rise; that unless you peel a cucumber from the end it doesn't grow, it will be bitter; that if you want boiled fowl to be tender you put a small glass bottle in the water with it; that two silver florins should be cooked with jam to prevent it burning; that egg whites beat better if beaten in the sunshine. Of course, egg whites then were not beaten with an electric mixer but with a silver knife on a flat plate, so taking them out into the sunshine was not all that difficult. You beat them until you were able to turn the plate upside-down without their falling off. And I've lost a good many egg whites that way!

I began this book for you because of the way I feel about cooking – because you were brought up in small kitchens, in big cities outside Australia – because I didn't want the recipes I had known and loved to be lost altogether – and because I wanted you to know at least a little of "what cooks" in Australia.

When I suggested I was writing an "Australian Cookbook" Australians generally were pretty surprised. They said that apart from damper and kangaroo tail soup, there wasn't any truly "Australian" recipe. Basically, I suppose most of those I consider Australian did originally come from England, but it seemed to me that if I ignored the probable origin and put together recipes which had come to me in Australia from Australians, I would be providing you with a sort of Heritage from Home to take into whatever kitchen you eventually preside over.

Many of these have come from the handwritten books which my mother, my aunts and my grandmother all kept, reading almost like diaries in their progression of names and places attached to recipes, and fascinating in their wealth of added instruction ("I always

A staff member and me (left) during a visit to a a YWCA
womens shelter in rural South Australia in the early 1970s.

♥ ♥

use apricot jam", "Ruby puts in two tablespoons", "Best if left in 10 minutes longer".) Of course sometimes there's just no instruction at all. One entry reads simply, "Breadcrumbs, dripping, time, parsely, nutmeg" – and the spelling is not mine.

In going through these books I found a large percentage of sweet things – jams, biscuits, cakes and desserts – and I'm not sure whether this indicates that my relatives were sweet-toothed, or that Australian cooking generally is sweet. It is a fact that when I ask for Australian recipes, my friends almost always offer something in this same category.

Apart from these old ones, I include recipes which I myself have collected along the way, writing them down just as my mother did – "Marjorie's Coffee Dessert", "Margaret's salad". A kind of gastronomic life history.

For this is the way tradition grows. The original settlers brought with them their own recipes, adapting and making do as best they could. Their daughters took those they liked best and grafted on their own ideas and discoveries, each adding her special touch according to the way her life went and her tastes developed. What is being added to Australian cooking now, of course, is a real international flavour,

♥ ♥

❤ ❤

as all those New Australians settle themselves into their Australian kitchen and look round to see what cooks.

The memories of your childhood cooking will not be as mine. You will remember things which I cooked for you and which were once cooked for me by my mother, though you may not have recognised them as such. But you will also remember the small oblong kitchen in 52nd Street, and the even smaller one in 63rd, where Helen and I tripped over each other as I fried the chicken and she made real American apple pie. You will think of the big square kitchen in Kensington, and the funny little Stanley Oven on which I cooked in India. (Do you remember how – no matter what I was cooking – Naraian would always come in and say hopefully, "Curry, memsahib?") I hope you'll not forget the Greek food we cooked at one time, the splendid and expensive results of my French period, nor the Swiss accent that has been added in Geneva.

All this is your heritage of cooking, and I would not be honest if I passed on to you just the Australian part of it. But this brings me to a very practical point. Measurements. Most Australian recipes – or most of the older ones anyway – list ingredients by weight. I haven't owned a set of kitchen scales since I don't know when, so this is a trifle awkward. I was brought up to believe that one tablespoon equalled one ounce, but it has

❤ ❤

been borne in on me through the years that a tablespoon of cornflour and a tablespoon of sugar can't possibly weigh exactly the same. However, it's a good basic rule, and I still work on it – sometimes with interesting results! Actually for a while when we first went to live in the States, all results were fairly interesting, until I realised that American and English cooks don't measure things the same way. In Australia now you can buy American measuring spoons, and I also found a "Cook's Aid" which indicates both English and American cup measures. For your convenience I have indicated wherever I have used other than English measurements. If you don't have the right equipment to translate these into English, there are one or two things you'll need to know.

An American cup is two tablespoons less than an English one. Both the American and the English cup equal half a pint, from which you'll gather an American pint is four tablespoons less than the English imperial pint. An American tablespoon is the equivalent of an English dessertspoon. Of course, if your recipe's French, then a "cuillere a cafe" turns out to be a teaspoon. Oh well, I think it's probably a bad thing in this life to be too careful with one's weighing and measuring.

Unless otherwise stated, most of the recipes I give are meant for four people. You must remember, however, that although both my mother and I basically cooked for a family of four, we usually also allowed for the possibility of something left over for the next day's lunch, an extra hungry child with a larger than normal appetite, or a stranger or two within our gates. I don't feel I can be specific to the last crumb as to how many these recipes will feed, but I have tried to indicate where they are planned for more than four.

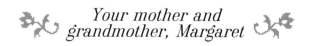

Your mother and grandmother, Margaret

*A recent picture of me, my daughter Kate (left),
granddaughter Noni (right), and the Easter Bonnet Pudding.*

PART ONE
first things first

AN ARTIST FRIEND OF MINE USED TO
SAY "I LIKE GOING TO DINNER WITH
YOU, YOU HAVE SUCH GOOD 'AFTERS'".
BUT FIRST OF ALL, ONE HAS TO DEAL
WITH THE "BEFORES" – THE STARTERS
AS THEY'RE CALLED THESE DAYS – AND I
DON'T REMEMBER THAT WE REALLY HAD
THESE IN MY YOUTH. OF COURSE, THERE
WAS FREQUENTLY SOUP OR FISH, BUT
THEY WERE JUST PART OF THE MEAL.
THE GROWN-UPS HAD A GLASS OF DRY
SHERRY BEFOREHAND, BUT NOTHING TO
EAT WITH IT.

♥ ♥

AS I GREW UP, I ALSO WAS ALLOWED A GLASS OF DRY SHERRY. (SWEET SHERRY, MY FATHER SAID, FROWNING ON MY YOUTHFUL PREFERENCE, IS FOR COOKING!) As a result, I have grown up with a firm liking for dry sherry, but no "family" recipes for hors d'oeuvres. However, both my mother and my aunt were great bridge players, and bridge parties provided a marvellous opportunity for producing sandwiches, which they did in endless varieties. I will never forget the two of them, sitting at the big square kitchen table, working on a sort of assembly line of sandwiches. The fresh bread, white and brown, was cut into thin, even slices for them by the local grocer on his meat slicing machine. It stood in neat piles at one end of the table to my aunt's right. Then there was the softened butter, and a variety of fillings, all lined up in their separate saucers. At the end of the line we children waited to eat the crusts, which were neatly cut off before the sandwiches were sliced into triangles, and to which some butter and filling always adhered. You don't find shops that will slice the bread for you now, and today's thick, butterless sandwiches bear little resemblance to those small savoury triangles. Always fresh, because they were stacked and wrapped carefully in a damp cloth until needed, and as good to the eye as to the palate, because as much care was taken with the colour as with the consistency and taste of the fillings. The finished plate was usually decorated with nasturtium, which grew in great profusion in our garden, the leaves and seeds of which are edible. Some of those fillings I still use as dips, or on crackers with pre-dinner drinks.

Sometimes mother would make a sandwich purely for her own consumption. If she were frying chopped onions, for example, she would do a few extra and make herself a fried-onion sandwich. This was purely for kitchen eating, never for guests, but I can recommend it. The crisp, brown, still-hot onions, between bread and butter, are delicious. A more elegant way of making an onion sandwich, which can be served to guests with their pre-dinner drinks, was shown to me in New York.

♥ ♥

ONION SANDWICH

Use the gentle white onions, which are not too strong, and slice them with a stainless steel knife into the thinnest whole circles you can manage. From thin slices of white bread, cut rounds the same size as the onion, butter them and place an onion slice peppered and salted, between two rounds of bread. The secret is to have it all very thin, and the sandwiches no bigger than about 1½ inches in diameter. Serve them on a plate centred with a bouquet of parsley or some small cherry tomatoes. They need a little colour.

WAYS WITH EGG

Hard-boiled eggs, of course, are a basic ingredient for fillings and spreads. Here are three ways my mother used them.

EGG AND MINT

Mash hard boiled eggs very smoothly with just enough mayonnaise to get the consistency you want. Add white pepper and salt to taste and then chopped fresh mint leaves. Heap on crackers, with a small mint leaf on top for colour.

ANCHOVY PASTE

Mix well together the yolks of two hard boiled eggs and approximately the same amount of butter, a little cayenne pepper and 1 teaspoon of anchovy sauce.

HAM SAVOURY

Pound ham in a mortar with one or two hard boiled egg yolks, a knob of butter, pepper, salt and nutmeg. This is what always happened to the last bits of a ham, and it makes a good spread. Sometimes a little bit of chopped chutney is added, and it can also be made with tongue instead of ham, if that's what you happen to have – or prefer.

CHICKEN LIVER SPREAD

One of the ways I have learned to use a hard boiled egg is with chicken livers. There is no rule for this one. As far as I know, it just came into being. There comes a moment when you have used two or three chickens but not their livers, so you are left with two or three chicken livers. What you do is to cook them quickly in generous butter – still a little pink on the inside please – pepper well, salt too and a little worcester sauce, maybe. Then mash them thoroughly with a hard boiled egg, getting it as smooth as possible. There is nothing to forbid frying a thin slice of onion in the butter before the chicken livers, or adding a touch of sherry afterwards, or brandy. Brandy gets along well with chicken livers in any shape or form. Of course, if you had half a pound of livers to cope with, you would need more than one hard boiled egg. You will just have to use your own judgment. Chopped chives or parsley are possible too. The only rule is that you finish up with a workable mixture that can be put on crackers. You will have no trouble in getting people to eat it.

LIVER PÂTÉ

Another liver recipe which came to me from one of "the young" who helped me with the Sunday Lunch Group at Holy Trinity Church, Geneva – but which I swear has American origins – is a quick and easy liver pâté.

- ♥ ³/₄ lb. liverwurst
- ♥ 2 oz. melted butter

Beat these together until smooth and add

- ♥ 1 level tablespoon chopped parsley
- ♥ 1 dessertspoon brandy (sherry if you don't have brandy)
- ♥ ¹/₄ teaspoon thyme
- ♥ salt and pepper

I was about to add "to taste" after that last, but then remembered that my lunch party friend, in giving me this recipe said, "For goodness sake don't taste it until it is chilled, or you'll never make it again". So I am not sure how you know about the seasonings. Put in what you think, pray to St Josephine, and pack it firmly into a crock or small bowl from which you can serve it direct and put it into the refrigerator overnight. A refinement I can recommend is to put over the top a thin film of canned beef bouillon in which you have dissolved a little gelatine – 1 teaspoon to 1 cup bouillon. If you want to turn it out, set the layer of beef bouillon first, top it with the mixture (which is very soft in the beginning) and then refrigerate overnight.

INGE'S CHEESE BISCUITS

Another staple for the hors d'oeuvres tray, of course, is cheese. The best way I know is in Inge's cheese biscuits. I used to have trouble with these in New York because there, of course, a "biscuit" was something else again, and you could hardly call it a cookie. But, nameless as they frequently were, they became justifiably famous at our 63rd Street "Dunnery". "Where are those cheese 'things' you always make?", people would ask me. I tried always to serve them very fresh – they smell so good then – and in a round silver bowl they look their best.

Inge, who originally gave me the recipe, came with her husband to South Australia during the war, so one may assume that these "things" are of Austrian descent. I decided long ago that since Inge and her husband now make good South Australian wine, I could classify the biscuits as Australian. Oddly enough, many years later, going through my grandmother's recipes I found exactly the same recipe, labelled prosaically "Cheese straws". They say current jokes are taken from continent to continent by air pilots, but recipes? Maybe they just float about in the air. (I had a friend in New York whose theory it was that if you lost weight, the fat that disappeared from your body had to go somewhere, and just floated about until it found some place else to lodge. It is my theory it usually lodged with me!) However, wherever this originated – Austria or Australia – it is well worth keeping.

TAKE EQUAL WEIGHTS OF:
- ❤ butter
- ❤ flour
- ❤ grated cheese – a good sharp cheddar

Add salt and cayenne pepper to taste, and work well together into a dough. Roll out, not too thinly, a little at a time because it is a very short dough and difficult to work with, and cut into small rounds. Brush with beaten egg and bake in a moderate oven. The dough can be made ahead of time and kept in the refrigerator wrapped in grease-proof paper, and cooked at a later time. It also freezes well. When rolling and cutting it, keep the dough as cold as possible, since otherwise, it is impossible to work with. Half a pound of each ingredient makes approximately a hundred small biscuits and (theoretically) they keep well.

Ever since you can remember, I have cut these into rounds with the silver whiskey jigger which belonged to my father, and which is used far more often for cutting cookies than for measuring whiskey. Alas! My grandmother's recipe says "cut into fingers", and Inge told me "put a few caraway seeds on top". I have ignored both these instructions, but maybe you'd like to try them.

MICHAEL'S MIXTURE

We once went by ship from London to New York with a young man who made his living by condensing books for the *Reader's Digest*. Despite this, he was a pleasant table companion and even if he hadn't been I'd remember him with gratitude, for it was he who taught me how to make these very simple hors d'oeuvres which have stood me in good stead over a number of years.

Take slices of salami, remove the skin and spread with softened cream cheese, stack them one on top of the other about an inch high, and ending with salami. Wrap in wax paper and store in the refrigerator for at least an hour.

When ready to use cut in squares and spear each with a toothpick.

You can do the same with any of those highly spiced sausages you find at your delicatessen – garlic sausage, mortadella, bologna. They are all good. If you use the large kind, such as mortadella, spread each slice with cream cheese, roll it up like a Swiss roll, wrap and refrigerate. Cut the rolls into 1/2 inch slices.

AUDREY'S CHEESE ROLL

Cream cheese has many uses. My mother used to make a cream cheese of sorts with any milk that happened to go thick and sour. (And before the days of the refrigerator in every kitchen, milk frequently did just that.) She warmed it very gently over a low heat until it "broke" and then hung it in a piece of cheese cloth to drip dry over the sink. When all the liquid had dripped out of it, she mixed it with a little cream, salt and cayenne pepper. Delicious, but simpler these days to buy it from the delicatessen. When you've bought it, here's one of the things you can do with it.

Grate 4 oz. of cheddar cheese and blend with 4 oz. blue cheese, and 4 oz. cream cheese. Add finely chopped walnuts, and form the whole into a fat sausage-shaped roll. Cover the outside of it with chopped parsley, and serve with crackers.

THE GREAT AMERICAN DIP

The cocktail dip is an American invention, or at least it came to me in that country. It is delicious though not exactly slimming. (My advice to you is just to rise above the thought of bathroom scales and enjoy yourself for once.) It gives plenty of scope for imagination and is a practical and satisfying thing to make, but there are three things you must remember. First, if your guest is standing with a drink in one hand and possibly a cigarette in the other, it is almost impossible for him to cope with a do-it-yourself dip. A good hostess will have some crackers already spread before she hands them round. After that of course she can sit it on the table and let people go it alone. Second, be careful not to make the mixture too thin, or it will be more of a "drip" than a dip and you won't be voted this year's best hostess. And third, for your own protection, when you set your pretty little bowl of dip in the centre of your pretty plate full of crackers, anchor it firmly. Otherwise, when you or an unsuspecting guest picks it up quickly, the dip is likely to go skittering across the plate and off onto the floor. You can avoid this by making a piece of masking tape into a circle, sticky side out, and pressing it to the bottom of your bowl before pressing that onto the plate. Copyright for this idea belongs to your father who at one of our early Christmas parties ... oh well, maybe you remember the mess it made.

BASIC CHEESE DIP

It's impossible to give exact proportions for this because the ingredients vary so much from country to country, but I use a mixture of one part cream cheese, to two parts cottage cheese and enough sour cream to get the consistency I want. Into this bland base go the seasonings. Salt, of course, and cayenne pepper. A little onion juice – scrape your cut onion over the cheese mixture so that it cries into it. Turn your head away so that you don't. A touch of garlic according to your taste. And there you have the base. Add to it what you will. Minced clams, if you're lucky enough to have them, but remember that even though you drain them well, they'll thin the mixture a little. So make it stiffer than normal. If you can't buy minced clams, try a small can of shrimp instead. Chopped stuffed olives are a good thing too, and so is red caviar. And a simple herb mixture – parsley, chives, tarragon, basil – depends what you've got and what you like. A good deal of tasting and trying is involved, but it's worth experimenting.

Whatever you put into your dip, remember that all those ingredients need time to get acquainted. Make it the night before you need it and don't do your final tasting until they've had time to do so.

Finally, see that the dip is as attractive as it tastes. A plain white mixture is not the most eye appealing, so a sprinkle of chopped parsley, chives, olives, paprika or red caviar not only improves the appearance but indicates what's inside.

ELEANOR'S AVOCADO DIP

I always feel I owe this one to the United Nations. Your father once showed friends of friends over the headquarters in New York and bought them lunch. As a result they sent us a present. It turned out they were avocado growers in California, and we received a whole case of avocados. They were the most perfect and most delicious I have ever tasted, but a case of avocados takes some eating. The books tell you that there are ways of freezing them, but I never had much success with this. I did, however, have great success with this recipe given me by another UN wife.

Mash 1 large avocado very smooth and add 1 teaspoon of lemon juice. Then mix it with 2 tablespoons of mayonnaise and 2 of sour cream. Add salt, cayenne pepper and garlic powder to taste. It is best served with potato chips, but not the fragile ones which break into bits when you try to dip them.

BRAIN SAVOURY

Brains are a very useful basis for sandwich fillings and for dips. Perhaps you should not go round saying so in a loud clear voice to all your guests, but brains, cooked and well mashed with a little cream, cream cheese, mayonnaise or lemon juice are a very good bland basis to which you can add other flavours. My mother used to pepper and salt this mixture well, add chopped walnuts and use it as a sandwich mix. I have served them as a dip with plenty of chopped chives mixed in. My aunt did it this way.

- 1 set lamb's brains
- 1 tablespoon cream
- 1 dessertspoon grated cheese
- 1 beaten egg
- 1 teaspoon chopped capers
- pepper, salt, stuffed olives

Cook and mash the brains well and add the cream, cheese, beaten egg, capers and pepper and salt to taste. Cayenne pepper is best here. Return to the fire and cook, stirring all the time until mixture thickens.

When cold, put on crackers, heaping it up a little and topping with a slice of stuffed olive.

I know there are many who would dispute my earlier remark about the cocktail dip as an American invention. There are other countries who have specialised in such things (even if not with cocktails) for centuries. And just to show that I am aware of – and grateful for – this, here are three of my favourites from quite another part of the world.

GREEK YOGHURT DIP

Dips – whatever their nationality – need a light rein. It is not possible to be too precise in directions. For instance, this particular one asks for a "clove" of garlic, and once, slavishly following directions, I used just that. Only to discover later that my clove must obviously have been very considerably larger than the recipe intended. Or stronger. Or juicier. The result appeared to be pure garlic. All other flavours disappeared before it. And so, I imagine, did my friends, until I'd finished eating it.

So keep an open mind about them and be prepared to adjust your thinking to circumstances. And when I say take a clove of garlic and mash it with a little salt, be careful. You need about the same amount of salt as garlic, but that also depends where you are. Salt is saltier in some countries than in others, I've found. However, mash it very smooth. Then take two or three shelled walnuts, chop them and mash them with 1 teaspoon of olive oil. I do this with a pestle and mortar, but of course you can use a spoon and bowl. It is easier if you chop them very finely first. When both garlic and the walnuts are reduced to a smooth paste, mix them into a cup of yoghurt. Add a little red pepper, and let the mixture sit for a while before tasting and finally adjusting your seasonings. Just before serving, add some diced cucumber. If your yoghurt is the very thin variety, I suggest you mix it with a little cream cheese to give it just a little body. It is a thinnish dip, but should not be completely liquid. I've often wondered about using sour cream instead of yoghurt. Maybe we should try some time.

BABA GHANNOUJ

This is an eggplant dip, and its ancestry is Arab. I understand its name means "Father of Greediness", and once you've tasted it, you'll understand why. It's hard to stop.

My recipe starts by saying take one large round eggplant, and I have always found this slightly difficult, for who knows what 'large' is in someone else's vocabulary. I take an eggplant weighing approximately 1/2 lb.

Prick it with a fork, and bake in a moderate oven until soft. This takes about an hour. Eggplant always takes longer than I think, and it needs to be good and squashy. Be sure to prick it first. I once had one that burst in the oven, and that put me off eggplant for a very long time. When it is cooked, take it out and plunge it into cold water for a moment. Then peel, mash and put into a blender. Chop and mash 1 clove of garlic with about the same quantity of salt, and add it to the eggplant. Now – and here comes the magic ingredient – you add "tahini", a kind of oily purée of sesame seeds – rather the consistency of peanut butter. If you look you should be able to find a little Greek or Lebanese shop to supply you. It is well worth a search. For this dip, you need 2 dessertspoons of tahini. Mix it with a dessertspoon of lemon juice, and then add it to the eggplant. Blend till smooth. Taste it and see if you need anything else. A little more lemon juice perhaps? A dash of red pepper? Even a bit more tahini if you're as fond of this taste as I am. When you are sure about it, spoon it into a bowl, smooth the top with the back of your spoon, and dribble a little olive oil over it. Chill and garnish with chopped parsley just before serving with crackers.

HUMMUS

This is first cousin to the above but is made with chickpeas instead of eggplant. You can, of course, start with dried chickpeas, soak them overnight and boil them tender, but I always use a tin, and these vary in size, so prepare to be flexible and have fun tasting. The amount of your ingredients may differ, but the method is always the same.

Drain the chickpeas, and put them in a blender with – for a medium size can – half a cup of water, the juice of a lemon, 3 dessertspoons of tahini, and 1 clove garlic, mashed smooth with an equal volume of salt. Blend to a smooth paste. Add a little more lemon and water if it is too thick to move properly in your blender. It needs to be very smooth. Taste, and add more salt if needed. The chickpeas seem to swallow up a good deal of salt. I like a little red pepper too. Spoon into a bowl, smooth the top with the back of your spoon and dribble a little olive oil over the top. Decorate with small pieces of tomato, or a sprig of mint.

Both these recipes are most easily produced with a blender, but of course they can be made without it. Arab kitchens have been doing so for a long, long time.

MUSHROOMS

Mushrooms are also very useful. My mother loved them. She used to say she never had enough of them, but at least once in her life she did. When I was about 11, we lived for a year on a sheep farm in the south-east of South Australia, and after the winter rains, the whole place seemed to flower with mushrooms. They popped up everywhere, and we could go out with a bucket any morning and come back with it full. I remember coming into the kitchen with my bucket of mushrooms, and huddling by the big black wood stove to warm my frosty fingers. Mother would take some of the largest of what I had gathered, carefully cut out the stem, wipe them clean, and then sit them on top of the stove, with a dab of butter in their middle and a little pepper and salt. We would wait till they sizzled a bit and then eat them, messily, in our fingers. They were delicious.

But they were the big flat field mushrooms, which taste delicious, but turn your stews and sauces quite black. They were the only kind I knew until I went to New York, and discovered the small, white, button ones, which I always suspected might be manufactured rather than grown. However, they too are delicious, providing you do not overcook them, and they have the virtue of not darkening your sauce. You can also eat them raw, which is how we served them with drinks.

Choose fresh, small white mushrooms and carefully remove the stem. Wipe them clean with a damp towel (don't dream of washing them) and fill their centres with a cheese mixture. You can vary this how you will, as long as you keep it smooth and make it tasty. I usually use cream cheese and roquefort in a proportion of 2 to 1, with pepper and salt and a touch of worcester sauce. Heap it up a little in the centre of the mushroom and top it off with a sprinkle of paprika.

♥ ♥

NEW YORK MUSHROOMS

Sour cream was one of the things I learned about in New York, and this way of using it with mushrooms is one of the most useful recipes I have. The quantities are so variable that I seldom bother to measure them, simply using whatever amounts I have. But if I were in a measuring mood, I'd do it this way.

- ♥ 3 or 4 spring onions or half a small mild onion, whichever is to hand
- ♥ 1 teaspoon butter
- ♥ 1 cup sour cream
- ♥ ½ lb. mushrooms, sliced
- ♥ salt and cayenne pepper

Slice or chop the onion and, very gently, cook it in a saucepan in the butter until it is soft. Add the sour cream and the mushrooms, sliced, and set it uncovered on the fire to cook. As the sour cream heats it will thin to a watery consistency and give every indication of remaining that way forever. But have faith. Let it bubble away steadily, but not too fast, and every now and then give it a stir with a wooden spoon. Just as you have given up hope of anything happening it will begin to thicken.

♥ ♥

♥ ♥

Continue to give it an occasional, friendly, stir until it has reached the stage of being not quite as thick as you require it. Then take it off the fire. Taste, and add pepper and salt if necessary.

It will thicken a little more as it cools. This is a most versatile concoction. Slice the mushrooms and cook it to a creamy consistency and it is an elegant sauce with chicken. Chop your mushrooms and cook it a little thicker and it makes a good dip. Chop the mushrooms really fine, cook it just a little thicker and you can either put it on crackers, or fill puff cases with it.

If – heaven forfend – there is no onion in your kitchen, or you have a guest who is allergic – simply cook the mushrooms in sour cream. And I don't think the actual measures are too important.

Only one word of warning. It does thicken a little after you take it off the fire, and if you have it too thick, you finish up with mushrooms in rubber.

♥ ♥

MRS OODNADATTA JONES' CREAM PUFFS

That's what they're called in my mother's book, but I am slipping them in here among the hors d'oeuvres because this is the recipe I always use for savoury puffs at cocktail parties, the puff cases into which I put the above mushroom mixture – or any other savoury filling I want.

When my mother married, she went to live on a cattle station in the centre of Australia, up beyond Oodnadatta. This Mrs Jones was a friend from those days. When I knew her, she too had come to live in Adelaide, and I remember her with warmth and affection for many kindnesses and many happy times. She is renowned in our family for these cream puffs and the best recipe we know for strawberry jam.

Put 2 oz. of butter in $\frac{1}{2}$ pint of water and bring to a rolling boil. Add quickly 4 oz. of SF flour. Take off and stir rapidly with a wooden spoon until a smooth paste is formed. Remove from the fire and when it is lukewarm add 3 eggs, one at a time, and beat well after each egg. Drop spoonfuls onto a cookie sheet and bake in a quick oven for half an hour. The original recipe says "this mixture makes 18 puffs", but of course those were big ones meant for cream. For the small, bite-sized cocktail party ones, use a very small teaspoon, and you should get approximately 60–70.

And while we are on the subject of choux pastry ... (of course it really is choux pastry, that recipe I have just given, even though I did not discover it until I was forced into a "domestic science" class. I was not too pleased with the discovery actually. I preferred it called Mrs Oodnadatta's cream puffs, and still do. I also learned how to starch and iron a gentleman's dress shirt – a piece of knowledge I have never had the necessity to use.)

However, as I said, since we are on the subject of choux pastry, here is another that is well worth trying. It came to me in a very roundabout way from someone who had been living in France and who, when she returned to America, was asked, in the open-hearted American way, to give a talk on French cooking to the PTA, Women's Guild, or Thursday afternoon group – I can't remember which. Anyway, this is one of the recipes she gave. I must admit, that for a long time I thought the measurements were extraordinary, but of course I now realise she was translating European grams into understandable American, and I am grateful to her.

GOUGÈRE AU FROMAGE

- ♥ 4 oz. butter or margarine
- ♥ 1⅛ cups water
- ♥ ¾ cup + 1 dessertspoon flour
- ♥ 1 teaspoon salt
- ♥ 4 eggs
- ♥ 2 cups grated Emmenthal cheese
- ♥ beaten egg

Heat the butter with the water, and when it starts to boil, take it off the fire and add all the flour at once with the salt, and stir until smooth. Put back on the fire and count until 20. (I've always liked that bit. It doesn't say so, but I am sure you should stir while counting.) Remove from the fire. Add eggs, two at a time, and continue to beat so the paste will have body. (This really is a nice recipe, isn't it? I am giving it to you exactly as I wrote it down one morning in Sewickly, Pa. oh so long ago.) Then add ¾ of the cheese. Make a circle of the dough on a greased cookie sheet, brush with beaten egg and sprinkle the remaining cheese over it. Bake in a 375°F oven for about 45 minutes. Cut it in slices and let your guests eat it with their drinks. Or serve it as a first course for dinner. Or with salad as a delicious lunch or supper. One of the nice things about it is that you can make it, arrange it in its circle on the cookie sheet, and then leave it in your refrigerator, nice and cold, until you are ready to take it out and cook it. It also freezes well.

Maybe this is the point where I should say that I once knew someone in America who, when asked for a cookie sheet, looked in the linen closet for it. Of course, it is what I think Australians call an oven tray or a biscuit tray. If you can bake cookies, or biscuits, or scones on it ... it's a cookie sheet. Don't worry with the linen closet.

Then, of course, there is soup.

We did have that in my childhood. Lots of it. Though I don't ever remember a recipe for it, and there certainly isn't one among all those recipes so carefully hand-written over so many years by my mother and my grandmother. I guess soup mostly just grew out of whatever was left over and whatever was to hand and whatever inspiration came upon you at that moment. One of you once remarked, "It is very peculiar, but whenever my mother cleans out the refrigerator, we have soup". Which was very observant of whoever it was. I guess it was not the same one who never did discover that the day she was so kindly let off eating vegetables for lunch she was faced with lovely vegetable soup for dinner.

I like making soup. If you do it in the haphazard way I remember it, there is a good deal of tasting involved, and the end result can never accurately be foretold. However, I have discovered through years of experimentation in this regard that there are some things which I know can go into the soup pot, although not everyone has thought about it. The last hard bit of cheese, for example, that got pushed to the back of the refrigerator and forgotten. A piece of apple. The leftover spoonful of green salad (but take out any avocado first). The scrapings of the chutney bottle. Bacon rinds. (Does bacon still come with rind in Australia?) The last of the wine. Of course, you do have to use your head as well as your leftovers. If you put half a bowlful of salad into the soup, it won't improve it at all. But a small amount of lettuce, tomato, cucumber and so on, with its accompaniment of oil, vinegar, pepper, salt and garlic, is a good addition. Actually, vinegar or lemon juice are frequently just what the soup needs to sharpen it up. A little grated lemon rind is also often a fine idea, and so is a touch of curry powder.

"What's this soup called?", you children used to ask when I had produced something absolutely delicious. "Soup" was the answer, for it really never had a name, and I don't suppose I could have reproduced it. But it was very satisfactory to make, and I still like making it. Though I must admit it is harder to manage as one's family dwindles. However, through the years I have discovered that there are soups with real recipes and real ingredients. I offer you the following.

"MY" SOUP

Frances has this written into her recipe book as "Mummy's best basic soup" and that's what it is – basic.

You start with chicken stock. Any cookbook will tell you how to make this. I make mine this way. I boil the carcass, neck, giblets, feet – whatever part of the chicken I have – with cold water, parsley, onion, bay leaf, celery, peppercorns, carrot and salt. I am not offering proportions. I don't think it matters very much. Obviously, if you have the bones of a very small chicken and enough water to cover it, you don't put in a pound of carrots. I never cook a chicken without making chicken stock. If I am cooking a chicken for a party, taking the meat off the bone so my guests can eat whatever I am cooking with a fork, then, of course, I make a large quantity of stock. If I am cooking one very small chicken just for myself, maybe I make just a cupful with the neck and the giblets (and the feet if that's the way the creature comes). I find so many uses for chicken stock that I hate to be without it. There is almost always some in my refrigerator, although there is a definite limit to how long you can keep it there. It will freeze, however.

I also know very well that if a recipe calls for chicken stock, and you don't happen to have any, you can use a cube mixed with boiling water. But there is something very satisfactory in having your own, sitting in your refrigerator waiting for you.

Well there you are, you have your chicken stock and in it you cook your vegetable, whatever it may be – potatoes, leeks, pumpkin, cauliflower (I once did it with those dark red carrots you get in India) – peeled of course and diced. If the stock is really well seasoned as it should be, you won't need any more pepper and salt. When the vegetable is cooked, tip the whole thing into the blender and blend until you have a thickish purée. To this add sufficient light cream to bring it to the consistency you want. Heat it gently and then start adding and tasting until you are satisfied with the taste as well as the consistency. What you add, in amounts according to your own taste, are nutmeg, mace, cayenne pepper, paprika and lemon juice or sherry.

The result is delicious. And the variations are enormous. If you use mushrooms, for instance, you will find it needs a little thickening. Beat one or two egg yolks (depending on the amount you are making) with a little cream and stir into the hot soup. Be careful not to let it boil after this addition or it will "break". If it does, of course, you tip it back into the blender and whip it smooth again. In some countries, the pumpkins are not the floury kind we have in Australia and America and so occasionally here, too, you will need to thicken with egg yolk and cream. One of the most elegant variations is to use a can of chestnut purée as the vegetable to be added to the chicken stock. You don't need to cook it then or blend, but do see that with the cream it becomes a nice, smooth mixture. I use sherry instead of lemon, and miss out the mace and nutmeg.

It is a good basic way of making iced soups too. For cold cucumber soup, cook the cucumber, seeded and chopped, and a little sliced onion, with your chicken stock. You will probably need to give it body with a little flour and water, but very gently does it – you don't want to end up with a porridge. Thin it with some cream and add a little grated lemon peel and mace.

For cold avocado soup, add the diced avocado to the chicken stock, blend, and thin with cream. Be careful of your seasonings because avocado has such a delicate flavour on its own, but a little cayenne pepper, grated lemon rind, nutmeg, and even a soupçon of garlic powder can do no harm.

If you don't have a blender, of course it's possible to rub the mixture through a sieve. Never quite as velvet smooth, but some people prefer it that way.

FISH SOUP

Not all soups begin with chicken stock – though I am afraid a good many of mine do – but a good cook should vary the stocks she uses for soup. Fish soup, needless to say, starts with fish stock.

If you are going to make this from the beginning, here is the best way.

Heat about an ounce of butter and ³/₄ cup mushrooms. You can use whole mushrooms for this or just the stalks or peel if you happen to have that. Add 2 teaspoons of lemon juice and shake over the fire for about 2 minutes. Then add 1¹/₂ cups of white wine, ¹/₂ cup sherry, 2 cups of water, and the usual accessories, onion, celery, carrot, a little fresh dill if you can get it, a bay leaf, peppercorns and salt. The fish bones I use for this are usually flounder because they are easier to come by, since most fishmongers sell fillet of flounder and must therefore be left with the bones. Three flounders are enough for this amount of soup. You certainly can make the stock with other kinds of fish bones if that is easier for you. Cook the whole thing gently for about an hour and strain.

If you happen to live in a small flat, making fish stock is an odiferous business, and therefore I have many times taken a short cut. In New York I sometimes used clam juice, although my friend Dione Lucas was horrified to discover it, and I have even been known to start with a packet of fish soup, heating it up as directed on the packet and using that as my basic stock.

However, assume you are starting with your own stock. Melt 2 tablespoons of flour, then add, stirring all the time, a cup of light cream and 2 cups of fish stock. Cook until it thickens, take it off the fire and then begin the tasting and adding process. What goes companionably with fish soup is sherry, lemon juice, cayenne pepper, paprika and mace. Sometimes even a little curry powder. And I do mean a little − not enough to be quite recognisable blends well with the whole, and so does a very small amount of tomato paste. When you have got the whole tasting the way you want it, add whatever fish you like − pieces of lobster, crabmeat, scallops, shrimps, what you will, and reheat. Beat an egg yolk with a little cream, pour a little of the hot soup over it, stir well and add to the saucepan. Stir it carefully but do not boil it again. A few chopped chives over the top add colour, and a small teaspoon of sour cream slipped into the bowl just as you serve it, is a friendly gesture.

❤ ❤

INA'S BORSCHT

Red beet was one of the vegetables we always had growing in the garden, and as a child I maintained they tasted like sour earth. But then we never had them any way except cooked, sliced and vinegared as a salad. I was about 18 when I first tasted borscht, asked for and was given the recipe, which was neatly written into my book as Anna's borscht. It is one of my proud boasts that I never lose recipes, and it's true that I still have some which I wrote down when I was 10 or 12 years old. I seem to have spent my life saying to people, "May I have the recipe?" However, we have moved many times since I was 18, and pages do come loose from well worn and much used books. Anna's borscht is – no, no, not lost – but temporarily mislaid. So what I am offering you now is not my first experience of this delicious soup, but a recipe which was given to me much later on. I am told it is the way borscht is made in Southern Russia where it should be eaten with black wheat – a refinement I've never been in a position to try – but since the friend who gave it to me absolutely refused to write it down, I cannot vouch for its exact authenticity. I can, however, vouch for its goodness and flavour. And of course, when a recipe is not written, one feels freer than normal to experiment. I've never found this did any harm at all to this particular soup.

❤ ❤

- 1 knuckle veal
- 2 cups shredded cabbage
- ⅓ cup each of finely
  shredded or chopped:
    onion
    potato
    carrot
    celery
    turnip
    tomato

- 1 piece shin of beef
- 1 shredded red beet
- black pepper
- salt
- 1 teaspoon sugar
- 1 garlic clove, crushed

Put everything in a saucepan, and just cover with water, then simmer gently for at least 1½ hours. Add 2 more shredded beets for colour and cook until they are done. Test for seasoning, and serve. Pass a bowl of sour cream separately. Good the first day – but much better reheated the next.

Or if you want a hearty keeper-out-of-cold, there's always

SCOTCH BROTH

I was not too fond of Scots in the kitchen, because I got sick of being told they had rosy cheeks through eating porridge, but I forgave them much when it came to this soup. The recipe is in my own book, written by a friend of my mother's, in a square no-nonsense-about-it hand, and describes itself with uncompromising honesty as "a practical version of H.V. Morton's 'In Search of Scotland' recipe". Just the same there's a certain whimsy about some of the instructions that I like. I like the end result, too.

The night before the brewing, take 1/4 lb. of pearl barley and allow it to soak in cold water till the morning. Do the same with 1/4 lb. (or, if you like, a handful more) of dried peas.

In the morning, take 1/2 lb. of best-end-of-neck mutton and put it in a roomy saucepan, covering it with cold water. Throw in 1 tablespoon of salt. Let it come to the boil and simmer for 1 hour. Take 3 leeks, 2 carrots, 1 big turnip and 1 young spring cabbage. Chop the carrots and turnips into small cubes, and cut the leeks and cabbage up small. Mix all well together in a basin. At the end of the hour's simmering of the mutton, pour in the soaked barley and peas and add the mixed vegetables. Stir well with a wooden spoon and boil 1 hour more. Prepare a handful of finely chopped parsley, and make a pink mush of 1 grated carrot.

At the end of the second hour's boiling, add the parsley and the carrot mush. Stir gently, and serve after another quarter of an hour's boiling.

VAL'S GAZPACHO

The first time I ever tasted this cold soup was in Val's New York apartment one hot summer Sunday lunchtime. Since then I have had it many times and seen many recipes for it. I am sure they are all good, but this is the one I have always used.

Grate into a mortar
- ♥ 2 fat garlic cloves
- ♥ 1 large onion
- ♥ 3 teaspoons chopped parsley
- ♥ 1½ teaspoons salt and pepper to taste

Pound it up!
Grate in
- ♥ 3 large ripe tomatoes
- ♥ 1 cucumber
- ♥ 1 large green pepper (of course you have removed the seeds and membrane)

Pound it up again!
- ♥ Add ⅓ cup olive oil
- ♥ 3 tablespoons vinegar
- ♥ 1 teaspoon oregano

Chill very thoroughly. Before serving add ½ cup of coarse breadcrumbs. Enough for four or five people.

From soup to fish. There seems to be a remarkable absence of fish recipes in my mother's collection, and yet I do remember having fish often when we were young. Mostly fried in batter, I think, and this was rather a sore point, because I always maintained I liked bought fried fish better than the home cooked variety which cannot have been very endearing of me. But the batter was different and I never knew quite why. I still don't but I have found a way which seems to me to come near to my recollection.

FRIED FISH

- ♥ 4 oz. flour
- ♥ 1 tablespoon vegetable oil
- ♥ 1 gill warm water
- ♥ salt
- ♥ 1 egg white

Mix the flour, oil, water and a pinch of salt into a smooth batter. (Be careful. This is one of the cooks who uses a wine glass, not a cup when she measures a gill. So add your water gently and don't make the mixture too thin.) Allow to rest for some hours before using. If it has thickened during this rest period, add a little more warm water. Immediately before use, whip up the egg white and fold it in gently. Dip the fish fillets into this batter and fry in hot fat. I think it is the oil, which my mother would certainly not have used and the use of the egg white only that gives this the crispness I liked so much.

Our fish recipes were definitely of the simple variety. My mother used to boil fish – or perhaps I should say she steamed it, for she used little liquid – but it was always simply referred to as "boiled fish". She took a large whole fish and laid it gently in a long pan, with some sliced onions, bay leaf, parsley, peppercorns and salt. Then she added the liquid, a little white wine and some water, and cooked it very gently. It was served up whole, head and all, on an oblong dish, with slices of lemon down its back and parsley around it. It was always accompanied by a white sauce, either green with parsley, or thick with chopped hard boiled eggs and capers. Later cooks refer to this sauce more delicately as a "cream" sauce but to us it was just plain "white" and my mother was very particular about it.

"There are lots of ways to make white sauce", she said, "but only one is the right way". You melt the butter in your saucepan, remove from the fire and stir in the flour with a wooden spoon. Put back on the heat for a moment and then stir in the milk, slowly, continuing to stir until it thickens, then add seasoning to taste. The right proportions are 1 dessertspoon butter and 2 dessertspoons flour, to a cup of milk, but obviously you will vary this according to the consistency you want.

FISH CAKES

Fish cakes we had too, sometimes made with leftover cold fish, and sometimes with canned salmon. I don't suppose there was a proper recipe for these – I think people just made them up with what they had, but the way I remember them is like this.

> Mix equal quantities of fish and mashed potato. Of course you have strained it if it is canned salmon and carefully de-boned it whatever it is. Add pepper and salt and chopped chives or parsley, then fold in carefully one or two beaten egg whites (according to the amount you have). Beat the egg yolks a little, and when you have formed the fish mixture into small cakes dip them into the egg yolk and then roll in breadcrumbs. Fry in hot fat until brown. These were always served with anchovy sauce and a "wet" vegetable like grilled tomatoes, cauliflower with cheese sauce, or marrow.

Adelaide is a hot place in the summer and in my recollection my childhood summers were hotter than most. I remember the relentless heat and the red dust which filtered in under every door, through every crevice. I remember the house shut against the heat, the blinds drawn to keep out the glare and we children flat on our tummies playing ludo in the dark central hall, the coolest place in the house other than the cellar. I remember the hot, heavy stillness of it all. Everyone was up early to try and get as much as possible done before the heat really clamped down. Nobody wanted to eat much. I imagine nobody wanted to cook much either.

One very hot day when appetites needed tempting, and my mother was finding the kitchen an unattractive place, my father took over and made Soused fish. We had never had it before, and I don't remember that we ever had it again. I wonder why. It was exactly what was needed that summer day, and I liked it so much I have never forgotten it. But even I must have been off balance with the heat for I didn't ask how it was done and I have been looking for it ever since. I think my father must have made it up. Nothing, of course, will ever come up to that delicious dish of my memory, but finally I have found something which at least comes near it.

SOUSED FISH

Cut the head off a large fish and put the rest of it in a shallow casserole dish. Cover the head with vinegar and add to it 1 small turnip, 1 carrot, 1 onion, all thinly sliced, 6 cloves, 4 peppercorns, a bay leaf and a little salt. Boil together until the vegetables are soft. Strain over the fish and bake in a moderate oven, basting occasionally, until cooked. Allow to cool in the juice, then refrigerate. Serve very cold with a crisp green salad.

SAVOURY CRAYFISH

One of the first fish recipes I collected for myself was for crayfish. It seems to me, we had a great many crayfish in Adelaide. Great big succulent ones, the best I have ever tasted. The fresh crayfish sandwiches we used to be able to buy from the Ritz across the way from 5AD, where I then worked, are a mouth-watering memory still.

This is one of the vague ones, but exceedingly good, and simple too. To a cup of white sauce, made the same way as my mother said, but using half butter, half oil, and substituting cornflour for ordinary flour, add 1 tablespoon worcester sauce and 3 tablespoons of hot tomato sauce. Hot in flavour, that is, not heated. Dice the crayfish meat and soak in the juice of 1 large lemon. Sprinkle it with about a saltspoon of cayenne pepper and tip it into the sauce. Bring to the boil stirring all the time. Pour into a shallow fire-proof dish and sprinkle the top with breadcrumbs, dot with butter and brown in the oven.

MOTHER'S LOBSTER NEWBURGH

This is one of my mother's recipes. I don't know that it is very different from other people's but it is simpler than some and equally as good as any I have tasted. Her recipe states firmly "fresh lobster", but I know she made it with crayfish and I have made it with canned lobster when fresh was out of the question. I have also used the same sauce for scallops.

- ½ pint of Madeira wine
- 2 oz. of butter
- seasoning
- 4 egg yolks
- ½ pint of cream
- fresh cooked lobster

Cook the wine, butter and seasoning for 5 minutes and then take off the heat. Beat the eggs and cream well together and stir very slowly into the wine and butter. Put back on a gentle fire and continue stirring until the mixture comes to boiling point. Cut the lobster into neat pieces, put into the sauce and allow to get very hot, but do not cook at all. Serve with hot dry toast.

Scallops were not part of my childhood, since they don't come from South Australian waters, and we didn't get frozen fish in those days. However, you can't marry a Tasmanian without discovering scallops and I had no trouble at all in learning to like them. (I had considerable trouble with that other Tasmanian delicacy, mutton bird, but we won't go into that.) The little nut-sweet bay scallops of America's East Coast are delicious simply sautéed quickly in butter, but your father liked his Tasmanian ones in a white sauce. They don't take kindly to long cooking, so the way you do this is to put the scallops into cold milk, and bring them gently to the boil. Then remove the scallops and set aside, while you make your white sauce with the milk. When this is ready, and it can do with a little lemon juice and cayenne pepper for flavouring, put back the scallops and the moment they are hot through, serve them forth. They are tender and sweet this way, not the rubbery morsels you sometimes get in restaurants, but if you want a really superior dish, then I recommend ...

MARJORIE'S SCALLOPS

- 1½ teaspoon brandy
- ½ cup lemon juice
- 1½ lb. scallops
- chopped parsley plus extra for garnish
- 2 finely chopped hard boiled eggs, plus extra for garnish
- small jar Danish caviar
- paprika

FOR SAUCE:
- 2 oz. butter
- 2 oz. flour
- 1 pint mixed milk and cream
- salt and cayenne pepper

Combine the brandy and lemon juice. Pour over the scallops and allow to marinate for 10 hours in the fridge.

Make a white sauce with the butter, flour and extra rich milk, salt and cayenne pepper to taste. Add to this the marinade juices from the scallops. Add it slowly, stirring all the time, or your sauce will curdle.

Butter a flat oven-proof dish, and cover the bottom with scallops. Sprinkle these with the chopped parsley and chopped egg, and mask with sauce. Repeat this until the dish is full, finishing with sauce.

Stand in another dish containing water and cook in a moderate oven for 15 minutes. Garnish with the Danish caviar dropped in teaspoonfuls on top, a little chopped parsley, egg and a sprinkling of paprika.

FISH FILLETS IN WINE SAUCE

There's always been a warm friendship between fish and wine. This one's even warmer, because of the rosy glow of port.

- ♥ 1 lb. fillets of flounder, haddock or cod
- ♥ butter
- ♥ 3 shallots, chopped finely
- ♥ pepper, salt and paprika
- ♥ 1/2 lb. fresh mushrooms, sliced lengthwise
- ♥ 1/3 cup dry white wine
- ♥ juice of half a lemon
- ♥ port

Wipe the fillets dry with a paper towel. Butter a shallow baking dish (a teflon-lined one is really best) and place in it the fish fillets in two or three layers, sprinkling each layer with the chopped shallots, pepper and salt. Dust the top liberally with paprika, and completely cover with sliced mushrooms. Pour on the white wine and lemon juice, and several dashes of port. Add 3 or 4 generous pats of butter on top and bake uncovered at 375°F for 15 to 18 minutes.

This is not a large amount. It serves two or three people comfortably, and what broth and bits of fish remain make a delicious soup for one or two of them the next day.

One summer not too long ago, I spent a week with friends in an apartment along the Greek coast, just beyond the Athens airport, where the great jumbo jets swoop in out of the clear blue sky, over the bright blue sea, and the passengers crane for a first glimpse of the Acropolis. It was very hot. In the long days, when the noise of the planes and the roar of traffic along the busy coast road made it seem even hotter, we could feel perhaps that the world we'd come to escape was still too much with us. But when we braved the torrent of traffic and crossed to the narrow, glittering beach, why that was something else again.

In the evenings, we ate there. At a small fish restaurant, full of extended Greek families extending happily and noisily way beyond the tables they were occupying, and waiters with no English but enormous good humour. There was the sharp insistent rhythm of Greek music from further down the beach. We sat with the warm, Mediterranean night wrapped around us and the soft Mediterranean waters sloshing about very somnolently below. And the fish we ate was the best in the world. Not complicated dishes by any means. But sometimes the simplest ones are best.

GREEK FISH PLAKI

Use 3 lb. or thereabouts of baking fish. You can use one large whole fish but I find it better to take thick slices of something like cod, haddock or halibut. The topping sits more happily upon its flat surface. But whatever you use, place it in a buttered oven-proof pan, and sprinkle it with pepper, salt, oregano and olive oil. Cover the top with thick slices of tomato and sprinkle over that a goodly portion of chopped scallion. Now take about 15 to 20 salted crackers – the kind you put cheese on – and crumble them. If they are the big square kind, and not the small cocktail-party ones, you'll probably only need 8 or 10. Use your good judgment and crumble them finely. With my fingers, I do that. Now chop a cup of parsley (I know it seems a lot, but it isn't really), and then chop finely (or put through a garlic press) one garlic clove. Mix the cracker crumbs, parsley and garlic together and spread it over the fish. Dot with butter and decorate the top with lemon slices. Finally pour in 1 cup of cold water carefully. Put the dish into the oven and bake for about 45 minutes. It tastes almost as good as it smells.

❤ ❤

This is one of the good things which came to me – along with friendship – from a little brownstone house on East 60th Street, New York, where Dione Lucas presided over an immaculate and well-equipped kitchen. It is a recipe I have used often, and always with success. It takes a lot of chopping, but there is no reason at all why you should not do much of this well ahead of time, wrapping each separate vegetable in neat little wax-paper parcels and setting it aside in the refrigerator until the moment comes.

DIONE'S SHRIMP CREOLE

Take 2 lb. of green prawns. Shell and clean them. Heat 2 oz. of butter in a pan, add the prawns and shake in the hot butter until they are well coated with the butter and have turned pink. Season with salt and red pepper. Warm 4 tablespoons of brandy, light it, and pour it over the prawns, shaking the pan a little until the flame dies. Take out the prawns with a slotted spoon, set them aside and then, in this order, add:

❤ ❤

♥ ♥

- ♥ 2 onions, finely chopped
- ♥ 1 large carrot, finely diced
- ♥ ½ cup finely chopped celery
- ♥ 1 finely diced green
  pepper and (if possible)
  1 finely diced red pepper
- ♥ 4 sliced mushrooms
- ♥ 2 large tomatoes, chopped
- ♥ ½ teaspoon finely
  chopped garlic

(Mrs Lucas was insistent that garlic should be chopped. I have been known to put it through a garlic press, with no dire results.) Season the layers with pepper and salt as you go. Then cover the pan, and cook, very slowly, for about 15 minutes, or until the vegetables are soft, but not mushy. Take the pan off the fire. Mix together 1 teaspoon paprika, 1 teaspoon curry powder, 2 teaspoons tomato paste, 1 tablespoon flour and ¼ cup of Bovril. Add 1 cup of chicken stock and mix smoothly. Pour this over your vegetables, put back on the fire and stir until it just bubbles a little, then slowly and gently mix in 1 cup of sour cream. Taste for seasoning. Put back the prawns and simmer very gently for 10 minutes. Serve with rice and a good green salad.

♥ ♥

A great fish standby when I was a child was tinned salmon. In those days I had never tasted fresh salmon, and I don't think it ever occurred to me to consider what the fish was like before it went into that tin. That's the way it was and that's the way we used it – cold, with mayonnaise and lettuce, made into a "loaf" with beaten egg and herbs, in fish cakes (but that was extravagant and we didn't have those often) or put into a white sauce and served with hard boiled egg and rice. I like it that way. I once had a glamourised version of this simple dish which went by the splendid name of "Salmon in a Golden Cloak" but the way I really liked it best was:

SALMON PIE

- ♥ 1 lb. tin red salmon
- ♥ 2 tablespoons butter
- ♥ 2 tablespoons finely chopped white onion
- ♥ pepper
- ♥ 2 tablespoons chopped parsley
- ♥ 4 eggs
- ♥ 1 cup rich milk, or cream

Strain the salmon, but keep the juice. Then melt the butter and sauté the onion until soft, but not browned. Put the salmon, and $1/4$ cup of the liquid in a bowl and mash with a fork. Add a goodly amount of pepper and the chopped parsley. Now that I live in Geneva I use fresh dill when I can get it instead of parsley.

It's a good addition, but we didn't have it around when I was a child. (Dill? What was that, for heaven's sake? As far as I was concerned, the boy next door. Now I know better, of course.) Add the onion, and mix it all well. Beat the eggs, and add the milk or cream. Cream is best these days because "rich milk" is not nearly as rich as it used to be. Blend the eggs and cream into the salmon mixture and pour it all into a pie shell. Bake for about 30 minutes, or until set. I know very good cooks who say that the pie shell should be partly cooked before you put in your salmon mixture, and maybe they're right, but I don't believe we ever did this. I normally put it into an unbaked pie shell, but it certainly works well the other way, too, and perhaps you will prefer it. If so, line your pie dish – an 8 or 9 inch one – with pastry, prick it, cover it with a circle of foil weighted with dried beans or rice and bake it for about 8 minutes in a quick oven just to set the pastry. If you do not pre-bake the pastry shell this way, it's best to have it very cold before putting in the salmon.

"MY" WAY WITH MUSSELS

Mussels are one of those things which are now easily available in Australia but which were not used much – certainly not at all in our kitchen – when I was young. There were oysters – as far as I am concerned, the best in the world – but not belonging in any cookbook. (For what should you do with them, but add pepper, salt and lemon juice and eat them, gratefully, with thin slices of brown bread and butter? Cook them? Heaven forfend!) But mussels. They're something else again. The recipe I have, and which I consider "my" way of cooking mussels, was given to me in New York and is written in my cookbook as Mussels Mariniere. I know now that this is a misnomer. It should really be called Moules a la poulette, but whatever its name, it's the way I like them best.

Put mussels* in a large bowl with cold water and sprinkle with a lot of dried mustard. Let them sit for 15 minutes, then drain and cover them with clear, cold water. Chop 2 small onions and a little celery, together with the celery leaf, and a small piece of carrot. Put this, with a large bay leaf into 1/4 cup of water. Add some black peppercorns and salt and simmer, very gently, covered for 5 minutes. Add to it 1 cup of dry white wine. Take the mussels out of the water and discard any which are open. Put them into the wine and water, cover, and bring to the boil, shaking the pan once or twice. Simmer for 3 to 4 minutes until the shells are well opened. The golden rule with mussels is – any shells open before cooking, discard, and after cooking, discard any which remain closed.

Put the cooked mussels into a deepish dish and keep them warm while you make the sauce. Let the liquid in which you've cooked the mussels boil rapidly for a few minutes to reduce a little, and while this is going on, beat 3 egg yolks with a good $1/2$ teaspoon of potato flour (cornflour if you don't have this) and 3 tablespoons of brandy. When well beaten add $1/2$ cup of cream. Strain the reduced stock onto this mixture, beating all the time, then return to the fire and reheat, but don't let it boil again. Pour over the mussels, sprinkle with lots of chopped parsley and serve with a good crisp loaf of bread and cold white wine.

* You will notice that I haven't said how many mussels. My original recipe said "2 dozen", but that's not enough for anyone. I use 1 lb. per person (sometimes an extra ½ lb. to allow for the open ones I have to discard) and I find I can use 4 lb. of mussels to the amount of sauce given here. If you use less mussels, well, you'll just have a little extra sauce per person (delicious!) but if you want to do more, then you'll need to increase the amount of sauce. In Geneva, I can buy mussels already cleaned, but otherwise, be sure to scrub them well before using. They're grubby little fellows – sandy too – and need a hard scrub and a good wash.

PART TWO
the middle course

MY FATHER LIKED TO GROW
VEGETABLES SO WE USUALLY HAD
PLENTY, AND THEY WERE SIMPLY
PICKED AND COOKED AND EATEN
WITHOUT FUSS. THE PROBLEM WAS,
HOWEVER, THAT WHEN THEY WERE
RIPE, THERE WERE A GOOD MANY
OF THEM — WHATEVER THEY WERE.
THIS IS THE REASON, OF COURSE,
THAT MY MOTHER'S BOOK IS FULL OF
RECIPES FOR MAKING TOMATO PICKLE
OR USING UP GREEN TOMATOES,
OR PRESERVING BEANS.

♥ ♥

I CAN REMEMBER MY MOTHER SITTING ON THE WOODEN BENCH OUTSIDE THE KITCHEN DOOR INTERMINABLY SLICING UP BEANS. She and my aunt had their own way of doing this. They did it on a board with a very sharp knife, slicing the beans diagonally and very, very finely. Nowadays, we like to simply top and tail beans and cook them whole, but the finer the better for my mother. They took forever and looked elegant, though nowadays we would say all the vitamins went into the water. This mattered less then than it does now, because the vegetable water went into the soup, so you got those vitamins somewhere along the line, I suppose. I was renowned for once writing a "poem" for someone's recipe book which began:

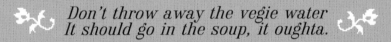

Don't throw away the vegie water
It should go in the soup, it oughta.

But enough of that.

My sister-in-law once said to me, "Why can't your brother cut up the beans like everyone else, standing up and slicing straight into the pan. He is the only person I know who has to sit down with a board and a very sharp knife". Old habits die hard. The way these elegantly sliced beans were preserved, as far as I remember, was simply by putting them in jars and covering each layer with salt. How I hated them. I never felt they bore any resemblance to the good, fresh, out-of-the-garden-this-morning ones. But tomatoes were another thing. And there were so many ways of using them.

♥ ♥

MR CUTLACK'S TOMATO PIE

This is the tomato pie we always have at Christmas. In Australia, of course, tomatoes are in season then so it isn't too difficult, but in New York it became an expensive tradition to produce this each December.

The recipe was given me many, many years ago by a scholarly old gentleman called E.S. Cutlack, who lived opposite our back gate and was a friend of my father's. He lived in the house from which, some years later, Frances produced a small, silent child whom she (Frances) assured us was called Joy Nobby Tonsil. After much inquiry we discovered that the surname was Thompson, not Tonsil, but we never did find out about that Nobby. However, E.S. Cutlack lived there long before Joy Nobby ever appeared on the scene. He was the first person I ever knew who kept a Commonplace Book. I was so intrigued by this that he gave me a shilling to buy myself an exercise book and start one myself, which I did. I filled it full of sad, romantic poetry. I have several recipes in E.S. Cutlack's fine, pointed handwriting, but this is the one that I have used the most.

Put alternate layers of sliced tomatoes, onion very thin, and breadcrumbs into a well-greased pie dish or casserole, seasoning them with pepper, salt and a pinch of sugar. On the top layer of crumbs put plenty of knobs of butter or good beef dripping. Bake until well browned, for 3/4 to 1 hour. Serve hot.

Although E.S. Cutlack didn't say so, I always peel the tomatoes first, and I put a few knobs of butter on each layer of tomato and onion, along with the pepper, salt and sugar. I have often thought a little basil mightn't go amiss either.

AUNT NELLIE'S TOMATO PIE

Aunt Nellie was my father's brother's wife. Our two families always celebrated Christmas together, one year at their house, one year at ours. I remember one Christmas when it was our turn to be the guests, my mother went out, locking up the house securely, and did not remember until we had arrived at Aunt Nellie's that she had left some soup cooking. She sat through the whole of that Christmas dinner without saying a word to anyone about it, because she decided it was no use worrying other people when there was nothing that could be done. Once my mother locked up a house, it was locked. She didn't stop at the back and front door. She locked everything, and she knew nobody could get in to turn off that soup. My father, when told of Mother's heroic silence, simply said, "If you had told me, we could have phoned the neighbours and asked them to turn the gas off at the meter", which was outside the back door.

I have often thought of my mother sitting placidly through that long ceremonious Christmas dinner, worrying like mad behind her calm exterior, but unwilling to spoil things for others. And all unnecessarily as it turned out.

In between Christmases, there was always a good deal of visiting went on between us. I don't suppose it was only lunches we had with Aunt Nellie. We must sometimes have been invited for dinner, surely. But yet my memory is of day-time visits. Of my father and my uncle walking round together inspecting the garden and comparing notes on tomatoes. Of a sunny, comfortable back verandah where my mother and aunt sat and sewed and talked. Of the dark polished wood of the dining room and deep comfortable chairs. And of lunches. The two recipes which I have carefully conserved from my Aunt Nellie's kitchen are naturally lunch dishes. And equally naturally, I suppose, one of them is for tomatoes. My mother once started a recipe book for my brother's wife, and included this with the notation "Dick is very fond of this". So am I.

- ♥ 1 1/2 lb. of ripe tomatoes
- ♥ 1 breakfast cup of soft breadcrumbs
- ♥ 1 large cup of milk
- ♥ 2 well-beaten eggs
- ♥ pepper and salt

Skin the tomatoes and chop finely. Put in a saucepan and cook slowly for half an hour. Add the breadcrumbs and allow them to swell in the juice from the tomatoes. When cool, add milk, eggs, pepper and salt. Stir all together and cook in a pie dish in a slow oven for 1 hour. Good either hot or cold.

Another thing we always had growing in the garden in great profusion, and which I would have preferred we didn't, was spinach. It was Kate who put my exact feelings into words when faced with a plate of this vegetable in New York many years later. She said, "Well, I can eat it, but I can't like it". Actually, I did learn to like it the way my mother cooked it.

She washed it well, cooked it in very little salted water, and drained it carefully. Nothing is worse than watery spinach. On top – and this was the real secret – she put butter, pepper, salt, grated nutmeg and a finely chopped hard boiled egg. And may I say here that when I say "finely chopped" that is just what I mean. There is a world of difference between a hard boiled egg roughly cut into 20 or 30 pieces and what I mean by "finely chopped". I want you to chop it so that the whole becomes a pale yellow mist, not a collection of yellow and white pieces. For some extraordinary reason, when properly done it always reminds me of mimosa.

TOMATO SOUFFLÉ

Not a soufflé at all, really. Not even a distant relative. But very good. Your grandmother used to cook it for me regularly for Saturday lunches long before I became her daughter-in-law. I never had the heart to tell her I didn't eat tomatoes (I do now) and when I married her son, she wrote it into my recipe book for me just like this.

Boil a cupful of macaroni in plenty of salted water until tender. Partly cook some rashers of bacon. In a pie dish, put alternate layers of macaroni, sliced tomato and bacon, with tomato on top. Slice them thickly. Beat up 4 eggs with a little milk, pepper and salt, and pour into the dish. Cook in a slow oven until set.

THE SQUASH FAMILY

Another thing we always had growing far more healthily than I would wish were various members of the squash family. I include in this apple cucumbers, which are delicate, crisp and delicious when eaten raw in salads or sandwiches, but definitely "squash" when cooked. And cook them my mother did. For breakfast. Covered with egg sauce, and sitting sadly on rather limp toast. You used not to believe me when I told you this, but it is true. Cooked cucumbers? you used to say. For breakfast? That's exactly the way I felt about them. But I had to eat them nevertheless, and years later when exactly the same thing was produced as a great delicacy at a fashionable dinner in New York I almost choked.

However, I have now recovered from my indiscriminate dislike of the squash family and find that many of them are quite worth knowing – preferably when very young, and never boiled. My favourite is what Americans call zucchini and the French and English (agreeing for once) call courgette. I think the downright Australians simply call them baby squash. There are also the small, pale green, scallopy edged kind which are equally delicious. Cook them this way.

In a thick saucepan or a small casserole put 2 oz. of butter, and melt it. On top put your vegetable. If it is zucchini, slice it thinly. If it is the light coloured "pattypan" squash simply remove the stem and put them in whole. Pepper them generously. Salt too. And a sprinkling of basil is a kindly thought. Put the lid on firmly and cook them on a very slow flame until done. About 15–20 minutes. No need to peel, and no need to add water. They will make their own juice, but should they become dry, add a very small amount of water just to encourage them.

Another way of using zucchini to advantage is in what Frances once nicknamed Rattatootie. Its real name, of course is …

RATATOUILLE

... and like most good things, you can vary the recipe more or less as you feel inclined.

The basic way I do it is to put equal quantities of sliced zucchini, diced eggplant and tomatoes, skinned and quartered, into a saucepan, together with two or three green peppers, seeded and cut in largish pieces, two big onions sliced, a crushed clove of garlic and some basil. Add to this 1/2 cup oil, pepper and salt. Cover and allow to cook slowly until it becomes liquid and bubbly. Then remove the cover and cook over a moderate heat until the sauce has almost disappeared and the whole is a delicious mush.

I am particularly fond of rattatootie served with roast lamb, and what's left over makes a perfect omelette filling for lunch next day.

Another vegetable I cook in much the same way is endive. Most Australians use this only in salads, without realising that it is also an excellent vegetable. It does, however, need a little more than butter to get it started.

Choose small, plump endive and cut the end off them. Put them in a saucepan with a small amount of salted water – or chicken stock if you have it – and squeeze of lemon. Allow to cook slowly, covered, for about 20 minutes, then drain. Put back in the saucepan, together with a large lump of butter, a little salt and a good sprinkling of black pepper. Cover and cook very slowly until done. Approximately another 10 minutes. Like the zucchini, they will make their own juice. They are delicious just like that, but you can also go one step further and make …

ENDIVES À L'ALBERT

I am not at all sure who Albert is, but I am grateful to him, for this is a most useful recipe.

After you have cooked the endives as above, drain them carefully and wrap each one in a thin slice of ham. Lay them side by side in a flat oven-proof dish. Make the white sauce with milk and juice from the endives, grated gruyère cheese to your taste and a dash of cayenne pepper. Sprinkle some more cheese over the top and brown in a hot oven. You can make this the day before and reheat.

It was Kate who used to ask, scandalised at such lack of sentiment on my part, "How can you possibly forget the names of the boys you used to know?" But it was also she who later came up with the statement, "There's no need to know a boy's surname unless you plan on marrying him". I honestly don't remember the name of the boy whose mother gave me this one, and I am positive we never considered marriage, but I do know his surname because it is written in my book as:

MRS MILLER'S MONK'S PIE

- ♥ butter
- ♥ 3 large tomatoes
- ♥ pepper and salt
- ♥ 3 cupfuls of mashed potato
- ♥ 1 tablespoon grated cheese
- ♥ 1 egg per person
- ♥ white sauce

Melt butter – a nut of – in a pan and add skinned tomatoes. Cook until they form a thick pulp. Season, add mashed potatoes and half the grated cheese. Mix all together. Pack the mixture into a pie dish and, with the back of a spoon make hollows as required, one for each person you expect to feed. Break an egg into each hollow, cover with well-seasoned white sauce, sprinkle with grated cheese and bake in the oven until brown and the eggs are set.

ELIANE'S GRATIN DE COURGE

This one's of a much later vintage. My father took great pride in his pumpkins. They grew and spread across a rather neglected end part of the garden, covering all its untidiness with green leaves and curling tendrils, with bright yellow flowers and eventually, great orange pumpkins. I liked the look of them, but was not so keen to eat them in those days. We called them Turk's Heads, and they were brightly coloured and rather cottage loaf shaped, dry and floury inside – a close relative of the Halloween type which makes pumpkin pie. Eliane's "courge" is a much wetter variety, more in the squash family I think, but her "gratin" works well with the other type too.

For four people, take 5 lb. of pumpkin. Skin it and cut it into dice and cook in boiling salted water. When soft, drain and wrap in a towel to take out the moisture. This is important! Purée the pumpkin and add grated gruyère cheese to taste, 2 or 3 eggs, a generous dollop of cream (Eliane says "une bonne ration") and whip all this together. Cook in a well-buttered soufflé dish in a moderate oven until well risen, browned and set.

SCALLOPED POTATOES

Scalloped potatoes are where a girl shows her versatility. You can vary the seasonings to suit yourself.

Butter an oven-proof dish – a flattish one maybe 2 or 3 inches high. Peel and slice your potatoes – according to the size of your dish and the number of people you are feeding. Peel and slice some onions too. Have ready, assembly-line style – flour, pepper, salt, butter and some herbs – basil, oregano, marjoram, thyme or parsley, whichever you prefer. Then get to work. Cover the bottom of the dish with a layer of potatoes and onions, then pepper, salt, herbs, a sprinkling of flour, and dabs of butter. Repeat this until you have reached the top of the dish or run out of ingredient. Be generous with the butter on top. Now pour over enough milk to come about $1/3$ of the way up the dish, and bake in a moderate oven for about 1 hour, or until the top is browned and the potatoes are cooked. Be careful with the herbs. You don't need too much, so sprinkle them sparingly, only put them on every other layer, or leave them out altogether. You can also leave out the onion if you like, I do, if I am serving the potatoes with chicken. Then, what I put between the layers is chopped parsley and paprika. You can experiment for yourself. There's an elegant Scandinavian variation known as Jansson's Temptation which omits the flour and butter, uses cream instead of milk and puts anchovies between the layers of potatoes.

"MY" JACQUELINE'S DAUPHINOIS

The Swiss have their own ideas and "My" Jacqueline gave me this one.

- ♥ 2 lb. potatoes
- ♥ pepper, salt
- ♥ 3 garlic cloves
- ♥ 6 oz. grated gruyère cheese
- ♥ 1/2 cup bouillon
- ♥ 1/2 cup white wine
- ♥ 4 tablespoons cream

Peel the potatoes and cut them into rounds. Arrange them in layers in a buttered plat à gratin – that's that flattish oven-proof dish again. Sprinkle each layer with pepper, salt, garlic (you have chopped it finely first of course) and grated cheese. Finish with cheese. Go gently with the salt, because sometimes the cheese is saltier than you think. Pour over all, the bouillon and wine. As in the previous recipe, this should fill about 1/3 of your dish, so the amount is a little variable. Bake for 50 minutes in a moderate oven; 10 minutes before it is ready, pour over the cream and return to the oven to brown. Serve it from the dish in which it is cooked.

BILL'S TARTE AUX TOMATES

This is one of those recipes which issued from that tiny kitchen on 74th Street in New York, presided over by a smiling Bill Vogel and his diminutive wife, Ruth, all through the years we were living a little further downtown on 63rd. Bill was certainly my greatest cooking ally in those days for, as much as I did, he loved to experiment, and nothing was too much trouble for him. He and I had splendid competitions in which we asked each other to dinners at which the rule was we could only cook dishes we had never tried before. I must admit some were better than others, but it was great fun. Bill was also one of the few people I know who feels as strongly as I do about cooking. And perhaps even more strongly, because whereas mothers, with conservative children and husbands on diets, do sometimes have to adjust their ideas to suit, Bill really could not bring himself to compromise with what he knew was the right way of doing things. Apart from his wife and his cooking, the great loves of his life were two Siamese cats named Elizabeth and Essex. The story goes that one day there seemed to be nothing much in the house on which to feed these pampered creatures. Ruth suggested that there was a chicken in the refrigerator. "I can't cook that for the cats", he said firmly. "I don't have any white wine."

Such a tiny kitchen. Such a large and generous cook. Such splendid dishes. This is one of them.

THIS WILL SERVE SIX PEOPLE, UNLESS OF COURSE THEY'RE FAMISHED AND THIS IS THE ONLY COURSE.

Make a good short pastry. Bill did this with 2 cups of sifted flour, $^1/_4$ lb. butter, 1 egg and a pinch of salt. I have been known to use my own recipe, but however you make it roll it out fairly thin and line a shallow pie plate with it.

Pour into this a cup of thick béchamel sauce, into which you have incorporated about $^1/_2$ cup of concentrated tomato purée.

Sauté in butter $^3/_4$ lb. chicken livers, which you have first shaken up in a paper bag with seasoned flour. Put these on top of the béchamel sauce together with a small can of pitted ripe olives. Cover with a thick layer of sliced tomatoes, which have been liberally sprinkled with basil and oregano. Top the tomatoes with thinly sliced mozzarella cheese and sprinkle with 1 tablespoon of grated parmesan.

Bake in a moderate oven for about 25 minutes until the pastry is cooked and the cheese melted.

♥ ♥

MARGARET'S LEEK PIE

One beautiful spring day when we were in Australia on leave, I was driven out into the soft green countryside beyond Adelaide to have lunch with Margaret. It was the sort of day that comes rarely and is not forgotten, warm with the touching warmth of early spring, bursting into flower all over the place. There were old friends, much laughter and a general feeling of well being. It was a perfect day. A perfect pie too, I remember.

FOR THE FILLING: MAKE A WHITE SAUCE WITH

- ♥ 4 oz. flour
- ♥ 4 oz. butter
- ♥ 1 1/2 pints milk

Flavour it well with salt, cayenne and a little nutmeg.

Add to this, 6 or 8 leeks, cut into 1 inch pieces and boiled till tender in salt and water, then well drained. Also add 6 hard boiled eggs cut in eighths, and 1/4 cup of ham. Put all this in a large round pie dish.

♥ ♥

FOR THE PASTRY:
- ❤ 6 oz. beef dripping
- ❤ 6 oz. plain flour
- ❤ 6 oz. SF flour
- ❤ 3/4 teaspoon salt
- ❤ 6 tablespoons cold water

Rub dripping into flour and salt, and add water, mixing with a knife, to a soft dough. Roll out about 1/8 inch thick and cover pie. Bake in a hot oven until pastry is brown and crisp.

With this, Margaret passed a bowl full of what I at first took to be a hollandaise-like sauce, but which turned out to be thick, rich, yellow country cream.

Under the same conditions as the previous recipe, this should feed six.

RICE IS NICE, TOO

I used not to think that rice was nice at all. We had it as a vegetable every week with the inevitable Sunday roast. Plain boiled rice, and I hated it. It seems incredible now but we also had roast potatoes, as well as sometimes roast pumpkin, so we certainly had our share of carbohydrates. In those days children had to eat everything put before them and so I ate rice. But under protest. One day I simply burst into tears and said, "I can't bear it. It's so sad. All those tiny grains". I think the family was fairly surprised, and even I have no idea what I meant. It created a slight diversion but I had to eat the rice anyway.

I still don't like plain boiled rice, but I have learned to like it very much indeed when it is dressed up a little.

SARMA'S INDIAN RICE

Sarma showed me how to do this one night in New Delhi just before we left India. We had all been sitting out in his garden relaxing after a long hot day of trying to get things packed and organised for our departure. The scent of jasmine was heavy on the still air. And there was also, from the kitchen, that sweet spicy smell of curry that is one of my keenest memories of India. It was very still, except for the quick movement of small lizards on the white wall of the house as they darted for insects, and the swoop of bats high above us. Nobody made much effort to move. Finally Sarma got up saying, "I'll go and see the rice". Then remembering my interest in all things culinary, he added, "Would you like to come and see how I do it?" Of course I would. Here's what he did.

In a saucepan, he melted a large lump of butter, and in this put four cloves. "You cook them till they crackle", he said, "but don't burn the butter". Into this, he tipped a cup of rice, stirring it around with a wooden spoon until each grain was well coated with butter. Then he added 2 whole cardamom, 4 peppercorns, and 2 cups of chicken stock. He brought it all to the boil, then covered it and let it simmer very gently for 25 minutes, by which time it had absorbed all the liquid and was ready to be stirred up lightly with a fork, and served. While the rice was cooking, 2 large onions were sliced very finely and fried crisp and brown – not burned but a rich even dark colour. It needs careful watching and stirring to get onions this way, otherwise you finish with some charcoal black and others under-cooked. Done properly they will come out crisp even-coloured rings which look good and taste better. Sarma spread them over the top of the rice and took the dish to the table.

RISOTTO À LA MILANESE

Even in the days when I didn't like rice, I liked this one. It was given to my mother by a friend who brought it back with her from a trip to Europe. I always thought of it as being an extremely exotic dish, because I was still at the point where I assumed that what you did with rice was boil it in salt and water. It had never occurred to me either that you could put other things with it. Even my mother must have thought it rather special for she wrote it down with its full "foreign" title rather than simply under the name of whoever gave it to her.

- ♥ 1½ oz. butter
- ♥ 1 onion
- ♥ 1 cup rice
- ♥ 1 pint stock
- ♥ pinch of saffron
- ♥ pepper and salt
- ♥ ½ lb. chicken livers
- ♥ 2 oz. grated parmesan cheese

Heat the butter and add the onion minced very fine. Cook but do not brown. Add the rice and cook for a few minutes, being careful that it does not burn. Add the stock gradually, stirring all the time with a wooden spoon. Partly cover the pan and cook gently until the rice is tender. Add the pinch of saffron, and season with freshly ground pepper and salt. Dip the chicken livers in melted butter, and grill them. Do not overcook them. They should be pale pink inside. Chop them in small pieces and add to the risotto. Serve with a bowl of parmesan cheese.

I must have been about 12 when this dish first made its appearance in my life, and as I have already pointed out it was a revelation to me. Quite apart from the additions, it was not the way rice was normally cooked in our house. Some 25 years later in New York City, my French cookery class set forth a way of cooking saffron rice which was almost identical. It is the way I now cook rice, willynilly, whether it has saffron with it, or chicken livers, or anything else. As far as I am concerned it is the best basic way of doing it.

SAFFRON RICE

Melt 1½ oz. butter in a heavy saucepan and add 1 finely chopped yellow onion. Cook slowly until the onion is translucent. Add 1 cup of long grain rice. Stir until the rice is coated with butter. Add 2 cups of stock or water. Crush ½ teaspoon shredded saffron in a pestle and mortar and mix it with 2 tablespoons of cold water and add to the rice. Stir until it comes to a rolling boil. Add salt and cayenne pepper. Reduce heat to a simmer.

Cover pan and cook, without lifting the lid, for 25 minutes. Fluff with a fork before serving.

DHALL

Sometimes for lunch, we used to have Dhall. It's a warming, economical dish we always welcomed and I wonder why I seldom come across it on anyone else's table.

- 1 cup lentils
- 2 or more cups stock
- 3/4 tablespoon curry powder
- 1 lb. onions
- 1 dessertspoon flour
- 1/2 teaspoon ground ginger
- 2 hard boiled eggs
- 3/4 teaspoon salt
- parsley
- toast fingers

Wash lentils and put in a saucepan with 1 cup stock and the curry powder. Simmer until all the stock is absorbed. Fry the onions brown, sprinkle with flour and stir to combine. Stir in the lentils with the rest of the stock, and the ginger and salt. Simmer until thick and tender. Garnish with the hard boiled eggs, quartered, parsley and the fingers of toast.

SLUDGE

And finally there is ... well that's what Frances called it, when she was small and that's what it has been called in our kitchen ever since. Maybe if you're serving it to guests you could think up another name. It was obviously borne of leftovers, and practically anything can be replaced by something else if that's what you happen to have.

- 1 cup uncooked rice
- 4 rashers of bacon, cut in strips
- $1/4$ cup blanched, slivered almonds
- butter
- 1 small sweet red pepper, diced
- $1/2$ cup sliced mushrooms
- 2 teaspoons lemon juice
- salt, cayenne pepper and paprika
- $1/2$ cup cooked chicken, cut in pieces
- $1/2$ cup cooked peas

Cook the rice according to the rules. Fry the bacon and set aside on paper to drain. Brown the almonds in a little butter and set them aside too. Fry the red pepper also in butter, but not long enough to brown it. And finally, the mushrooms. There's a right way to cook mushrooms and now seems to be the moment to tell you about it. Put two tablespoons of butter in a frying pan, and when it is foaming hot throw in your $1/2$ cup of sliced mushrooms. Shake the pan so they are all nicely buttered, then add the lemon juice, a little salt, pepper and paprika, and shake over the fire for not a second longer than 3 minutes. Most people cook mushrooms far too long, and it is sad, because they taste so much mushroomier this way. Remember, however, that I am talking about the little white button ones, not field mushrooms.

But back to our sludge. When the rice is cooked, use a fork to stir in gently all the other ingredients. Taste for seasoning. Let it heat through and serve. A good green salad goes companionably.

PART THREE
meat and right

MY GRANDMOTHER, MY MOTHER, MY AUNT, MYSELF – ALL OUR COOKBOOKS ABOUND IN MEAT RECIPES. ONE CAN ONLY ASSUME AUSTRALIANS WERE VERY FOND OF MEAT. AND STILL ARE, I THINK. A FEW YEARS AGO WHEN I WAS IN AUSTRALIA FOR SOME TIME, I USED TO BE VISITED BY A SMALL GIRL WHO LIVED DOWN THE ROAD. I DIDN'T KNOW HER FAMILY AT ALL, AND SHE CAME MAINLY TO SEE MY DOG WITH WHOM SHE HAD MADE FRIENDS THROUGH THE GATE ON HER WAY TO SCHOOL EVERY DAY.

♥ ♥

HER NAME WAS KATIE AND SHE MUST HAVE BEEN ALL OF 8 YEARS OLD. ONE SUNDAY SHE TOLD ME THEY'D HAD LEG OF LAMB FOR DINNER. Then her eyes misted over with the retrospective enjoyment of a gourmet remembering an absolutely marvellous meal and after a moment she said, rather wistfully, "You know how it is when you haven't had roast lamb for a couple of weeks".

Sunday dinner was always a roast. And none of your fancy foreign ways either. But good, plain roast dinners. Beef with Yorkshire pudding and horseradish sauce. Lamb with mint sauce. Pork with its crackling crisp and bubbly and its accompaniment of apple sauce. Sometimes chicken with bread sauce – the sort of chicken you don't seem to get anymore – big enough to be properly carved, juicy, and full of stuffing. There never seem to have been recipes for these things. You learned to do them from your mother, simply by being in the kitchen (and where else would the daughter of the house be on a Sunday morning with a roast dinner to cook?). I sat at a corner of the table and peeled potatoes or podded peas or chopped the mint for the mint sauce when I was older and could be more or less relied upon not to chop my fingers at the same time. And while I sat and worked away I watched and learned. I *knew* that my mother rubbed the rind of the pork with oil and started it in a very hot oven to make it crackle. I *knew* what time she put the beef in, so that it ran red when she carved it at 1 o'clock. ("Do you want some of the red gravy?", she would ask as she passed the plate. Yes, please!) I noticed that she always put lemon with her veal, and how she stuffed the chicken. This was not knowledge you acquired from books.

But we did not live on Sunday roasts, of course, and there were recipes for other things.

♥ ♥

STEAK AND PICKLED WALNUTS

I have had this recipe for so long, I don't remember where I got it. I have never eaten it anywhere but in my own house, and it is one of the things which I have produced "in foreign parts" when I wanted to offer something Australian. The only recipe I have found, which is at all similar appeared in the *Goulburn Cook Book* published in Sydney in 1911, and that finishes with what seems to me to be a rather off-putting statement – "This is very nice if carefully prepared".

My recipe is not only very nice but is very easily prepared. And the result is anything but off-putting.

- 1 1/2 lb. steak
- flour
- pepper and salt
- beef dripping
- forcemeat balls
- 4 pickled walnuts
- 1 wine glass of walnut vinegar
- 1/2 oz. butter
- parsley

Cut the meat into neat pieces and dip in seasoned flour. Melt a little dripping in a pan and brown the forcemeat balls. Then take them out with a slotted spoon and leave to drain on paper. Brown the meat well in the same pan, and put it into a casserole with 1/2 pint of cold water. Simmer gently for 20 minutes or until the meat is nearly tender. Drain off the gravy and boil it rapidly for 5 minutes, then add to it the walnuts cut in pieces and the vinegar. Knead the butter and 1 teaspoon of flour together and drop it in small pieces into the gravy, stirring until it boils and thickens. Pour over the meat, add the forcemeat balls and simmer for 20 minutes longer or until the meat is tender. Serve very hot, with a garnish of chopped parsley. My recipe gives no suggestion for making the forcemeat balls, but I do this by mixing together breadcrumbs, finely chopped ham or bacon, chopped parsley, chives, thyme, pepper and salt, and binding it together with an egg. I roll the mixture into about 8 small balls and brown them as the recipe says. This, obviously, can be varied as the mood takes you. Sometimes I omit the chives and use very finely chopped onion, sautéed first in a little butter. Sometimes I add lemon rind. As long as the mixture is savoury and well seasoned I don't think it matters.

The casserole goes well with mashed potatoes, noodles or rice, and it is excellent for buffet suppers.

COUSIN DAISY'S CORNISH PIE

My Cousin Daisy (she was my father's cousin really but we were brought up to address that generation as "Cousin") was a little woman with white hair, very blue eyes and a wonderful sense of humour. She was also one of the best cooks I have ever known and is as much responsible for my love of cooking as anyone else. Towards the end of the Depression when life was difficult and uncertain for my own family, I was sent to stay for several months with her in the small country town where she lived. She had one of those great big Australian houses built for the heat, with a verandah all round and a passage running straight from front door to back. The kitchen was right at the back, and my recollection is that it was separated a little from the house so that you had to go outside to get to it, but perhaps I am wrong. I do remember though, its brick floor, its big scrubbed table, and the great wood stove, from which so many good things came. I learned a lot from my Cousin Daisy – and not only in the kitchen. She was a wonderful person.

Since 1932, I have cherished a little book put out by the First Riverton Girl Guide Company simply because it contains the recipe for Cousin Daisy's own special Cornish Potato Pie. This is how she made it.

> Slice 1 lb. of good beef steak across, cut into pieces about 2 inches square. Place a small piece of fat on each square and roll up. Stand the pieces end up in a pie dish. Sprinkle with flour, pepper and salt (be generous with the pepper and salt) and just cover with cold water. Peel small potatoes and cover meat with them as closely as possible. Put a few pieces of fat, or the outside skin left over from the steak on top, and bake 1½ to 2 hours or until the potatoes are well cooked and brown. The water should not cover the potatoes, and should the gravy boil away fill up with boiling water.

DUNN'S FAMOUS HOT POT

My brother-in-law gave me this recipe on condition that I did not show it to his mother. His mother was extremely fond of it, but never knew exactly what went into it. "I don't know what he puts in to make it taste so different", she said. What "he" put in was a clove of garlic which was something his poor mother always maintained she didn't eat, and certainly would not have eaten had she known. This makes quite a lot as you will see from the ingredients, but it keeps well, or if you want less, make half-quantity.

- ♥ $2^1/_2$ lb. lamb chops (not the best loin ones you would grill, but neck, shoulder or leg chops, what you will)
- ♥ 2 oz. butter
- ♥ 1 cup of wine
- ♥ $2^1/_2$ cups beef stock
- ♥ 1 garlic clove
- ♥ pepper and salt
- ♥ $2^1/_2$ tablespoons flour
- ♥ 5 rashers of bacon
- ♥ parsley

Sauté the chops in the butter and then leave them to marinate in the wine for at least an hour. Then put in saucepan with stock, wine, garlic, pepper and salt, and cook very slowly for 1 to $1^1/_2$ hours. Thicken the gravy with flour and a little water. Fry the bacon and chop into small pieces and top with the parsley.

In the Dunn household, this was always served with carrots and onions which had been cooked separately and then put on top. The wine they used was a white muscat, but I prefer red wine.

MY FATHER'S HOT POT

My father had a way of making a hot pot too, which was simpler than the previous recipe, but very good. Most of the meat recipes I remember from my childhood turn out to be very simple with the good honest taste of the meat and vegetables that went into them, unmasked by complicated sauces or sophisticated spices. I suppose they are what are now referred to as "hearty" dishes. I have nothing at all against subtle sauces, and delicate flavourings, but I do remember things like this with the utmost affection.

In a deep glass Pyrex dish, put neck of lamb chops, sliced onions and sliced potatoes, layer upon layer until the dish is full, dusting the lamb with a little flour, each layer with salt, plenty of pepper and a little chopped parsley. Add enough cold water to come about a quarter way up the dish (this is why it is a glass dish, so you can see what you are doing). Cook very slowly for about 1½ hours or until the meat is tender and the vegetables cooked. Add a little more boiling water during the cooking if there does not seem to be enough juice.

AUNT NELLIE'S VEAL PIE

This is the second of those luncheon dishes I remember so well.

- ❤ 1½ lb. veal
- ❤ 1 lb. ham

Cut into small squares and put into saucepan with water to cover, pepper, salt (go easy on the salt because the ham is salty) and parsley. Cook slowly, covered, until the meat is tender, then thicken with a little cornflour and water. Pour into a pie dish and add 2 hard boiled eggs cut in four. Cover with good short crust, make a couple of knife holes in it to let the steam escape and bake in a quick oven until the pastry is done.

SHORT CRUST

Perhaps this is the moment to talk about short crust. There is always the possibility, of course, of simply buying a box or a frozen packet and following instructions, and I have nothing against this. But comes the time when you may want – or need – to make it yourself. Some recipes which call for short crust give their own particular way of making it, but my basic method is this.

Into 6 oz. flour with a little salt added, rub 4 oz. lard. The lard should be cold and you rub it in carefully with the tips of your fingers so you finish up with something that looks like fine breadcrumbs. Add to this – cutting it in with a knife – sufficient cold water to make a workable dough. Be careful not to add too much – a little at a time. Turn onto a floured board – my mother always used a pastry cloth, but I haven't seen one in years and I have a feeling the table top or a board is more hygienic – and press or roll out as desired. But gently, gently – pastry doesn't like handling.

Not quite so simple and certainly more extravagant, though coming from about the same period in my life is ...

THE CONTESSA'S BEEF BURGUNDY

When I was quite small, a titled Viennese lady came to Adelaide and gave cooking demonstrations to which my mother went. She brought home a little paper-covered book of recipes which, now very tattered and torn, I still treasure. This is the book of which I once told Kate, who was being superior about its rather grubby condition, "I might just possibly leave it to you in my will – if you behave yourself". I have many more complicated recipes for Beef Burgundy but this is the best. It is excellent for parties because it has to be made the day before, and is also remarkably good cold.

Cut into cubes, 2 lb. of good steak. Roll in flour and fry in butter until brown. Remove from the pan and add 1 1/2 large onions finely minced – fry golden brown. Peel and seed 1 1/2 lb. of tomatoes and add to the onions. Let this reduce and thicken, then add 1 1/2 pints of Burgundy. Bring to the boil and add 1 lb. of thinly sliced carrots, the browned beef and a veal knuckle, also, salt, freshly ground pepper and a few cloves. Simmer for 2 hours and allow to stand until the next day. Then simmer for a further 1 or 2 hours. Serve with spaghetti. Enough for six to eight people.

HUNGARIAN VEAL

I tell you, New York was where I discovered sour cream and all its myriad uses. It has a strong affinity with veal, and here is a dish which just goes to show you can get more out of the PTA than just paying your dues. It comes from the Rudolph Steiner School in New York.

Blend 1/4 cup flour with 1 1/2 teaspoons salt and 1/8 teaspoon pepper and rub it into 1 1/2 lb. veal steak, cut into cubes. Brown the meat in a 1/4 cup of hot fat. Add 3/4 tablespoon paprika, 1 sliced onion and 1/2 cup water. Cover and simmer for 30 minutes. Add 1 cup sour cream and heat until sauce bubbles. Add 1/2 cup blanched, sliced almonds, 1 tablespoon poppy seeds, 2 cups cooked noodles. Heat and serve.

VEAL VERONIQUE

Here is the recipe I always use for this classic dish – simple and good.

- ♥ 1 lb. veal steak
- ♥ butter
- ♥ 1 teaspoon chopped chives
- ♥ 1 teaspoon flour
- ♥ pepper and salt, milk
- ♥ 1/2 lb. green grapes
- ♥ 1/2 cup cream
- ♥ 1/2 cup dry white wine

Beat veal steak out thinly and cut into pieces. Brown in pan with butter and chives. Remove meat, and add to pan the flour, pepper, salt and enough milk to make a thick sauce. Add peeled and seeded grapes. Put back the veal and simmer slowly until it is tender. My recipe says "for about 2 hours" but I don't find it always takes that long. Cook it very gently though, and when it is done, add the cream and wine. Reheat but do not cook after this addition. It serves two to three people.

My aunt's book was full of recipes calling for minced steak. The one we had most often was Mrs Brett's Aberdeen Sausage. Neither a sausage, nor I daresay from Aberdeen, but good nonetheless. Usually eaten cold, with salad or in sandwiches.

ABERDEEN SAUSAGE

To each pound of steak (topside) use 3¾ lb. of lean bacon, and put through the mincer. Add to this, 2 cups of soft breadcrumbs, 1 nutmeg, grated, 1 dessertspoon of worcester sauce, 1 egg, beaten and 1 small ½ cup of milk. Put into a basin and steam for 3 hours.

MARJORY'S GRANDMA'S ROLL

This wasn't my grandma. I rather doubt that she was Marjory's either, for I have a feeling our grandmas didn't mess about with packets of chicken noodle soup. Though there is something very grandma-like in that extraordinary amount of green pepper (I once worked this out as being 6 level teaspoons, but normally I just guess). And there is a very homey, olde worlde flavour to "scald your pudding cloth". In any case, this is highly recommended, though not if you are in a hurry for a quick meal.

The pudding cloth, in my mother's day, was made of a square of unbleached calico, and was kept, between uses, washed and neatly folded on the shelf in the linen cupboard. The result was that it was always being brought out by mistake by whoever was sent to get clean tea towels. (No, no, dear, that's the pudding cloth!) Not having quite as much constant need for a permanent pudding cloth as my mother, I soon realised that a piece of old sheet did just as well as unbleached calico – providing, of course, that it wasn't so old and thin that it let the water in. Soggy pudding is no fun at all. Whatever you use, however, you first have to scald it – pushing it into the saucepan of boiling water in which you are then going to cook your pudding, and heaving it out again with the handle of the wooden spoon. A hot and hazardous procedure, and I've never been quite certain what the purpose was, but all the best cooks agree that pudding cloths must be scalded, and who am I to disagree?

- ♥ 1 pkt. chicken noodle soup
- ♥ 2 lb. minced steak
- ♥ 1¹/₃ cup soft breadcrumbs
- ♥ 1 large onion
- ♥ 1 clove chopped garlic
- ♥ 1 tablespoon worcester sauce
- ♥ ¹/₂ lb. lean shoulder bacon
- ♥ pepper and salt to taste
- ♥ ¹/₄ cup finely chopped green pepper (Oh Grandma!)
- ♥ 2 eggs
- ♥ fine dried breadcrumbs

Make up the soup, using only 1¹/₂ cups of water, and let it cool. Mix together the steak, soft breadcrumbs, cooled soup, grated onion, garlic, worcester sauce, finely chopped bacon (rind removed, of course), pepper, salt and that chopped green pepper. Beat the eggs and add, mixing very well. With floured hands, form into a roll. Scald your pudding cloth, flour it and wrap the roll tightly in it, tying it securely at both ends and pinning it in the middle so no water can get in. Put it on a rack in a large boiler filled with plenty of boiling water. Be sure the water is boiling when the roll goes in. Simmer it gently for 2 hours.

Do not lift the lid until halfway through the cooking time, then gently turn the roll over, put back the lid and continue cooking. Let cool in the water, lift out – careful not to break it – remove cloth and roll in the fine breadcrumbs. Chill before serving.

If you make this into a long sausage-type roll – which is its usual form – the easiest thing to cook it in is one of those large covered roasting pans – and maybe you will find it necessary to sit it on two low burners in order to keep it bubbling gently. I expect Grandma had a wood stove.

SHEEP'S HEAD PIE

This is one of the oldest of my recipes. I don't remember a time when my mother didn't make it, and if you have a cooperative butcher you can make it too. Someone has suggested you may also need a strong stomach, but as far as I am concerned, it is not nearly as bad as, for instance, dealing with a live lobster, which always makes me blanch. But you do need to get round your butcher, for while sheep must still have heads, butchers apparently don't seem to be buying them these days.

They will if you persist, however, and it is well worth the trouble.

What you want is one sheep's head. It comes split in half and complete with one set of brains and one tongue. Wash the head in salted water. Soak the brains in salt and water, skin them and cook in the usual way. Set them aside. Put the head and the tongue into a large pan with enough salted water to cover. Add to it all the usual soupy things, peppercorns, bay leaf, parsley, a large carrot, an onion, a turnip and a handful of pearl barley. My mother's recipe says to boil for 3 hours, but it depends on the size of the head. You need to cook it until the meat and the tongue are tender but not until it all falls apart. Take the head out of the broth when it is cooked, and allow to cool a little. Then take all the meat off it, and chop it up. Skin the tongue and cut that up finely too. Chop the already cooked brains and mix all these three things together with plenty of chopped parsley, salt and a good deal of pepper. Moisten it with some of the broth, but don't make it too wet. Butter a shallow dish. My mother, of course, used what was called a pie dish – an oblong enamelled dish about 2 or 3 inches deep, she had a whole nest of them – and this is why it is called a pie, despite its lack of pastry. I cook it in a small shallow casserole dish, but I still consider it a pie. Whatever you cook it in, butter the dish first, then spoon in a layer of the meat, sprinkle with breadcrumbs (the dried variety) and dot with butter. Then another layer of meat, another of breadcrumbs and butter, and so on until all is used. Finish with breadcrumbs and butter, then pop the whole lot in a moderate oven and bake until the top is brown. What you've got left in your saucepan, of course, is good, nourishing barley broth for next day's lunch.

PRESSED MEAT

Another old one for which you may need your butcher's goodwill is this from my Cousin Daisy. It is something we often had on summer Sunday nights when I stayed with her, a light, cold meal before going off to Evensong. During the week, she cooked enormous midday meals for some of the teachers and pupils who came in from neighbouring towns to go to the local high school, but Sunday was a day of rest. We had grilled chops for midday dinner, and fresh fruit salad, and in the evening we walked off together down the long main street to the Anglican Church, whose bell beckoned us all the way, saying "Come. Come. Come". (The bell at the Methodist Church on the other hand said very clearly, and rather sharply I thought, "Come along. Come along".) What we ate before we left had to be quick, easy and preferably made the day before. This filled the bill.

Take the flap end of a fore-quarter of mutton, crack the bones, roll and tie with string. My Cousin Daisy got this from her own farm, so it was easy, but your butcher can oblige. Place in a saucepan with onion, turnip, parsnip, carrot, pepper and salt, and a pinch of mixed herbs. Cover with water, bring to the boil and simmer until the meat will slip easily from the bones. Remove bones and roll the meat again. Put it on a dish, cover with a plate and put a weight on top. Leave overnight. Serve sliced, with salad. Once again, you are left with good vegetable soup on hand.

MOTHER'S SAVOURY STEAK

My father was of the opinion that provided you cooked steak with plenty of onion, for a long time, very slowly, you came up with delicious stew. You do too, but sometimes it is good to vary it, and Mother had her own way.

- 1 tablespoon flour
- 1 teaspoon sugar
- pepper and salt
- grated nutmeg
- 2 lb. steak
- 1 teaspoon vinegar
- 1 teaspoon worcester sauce
- 1 tablespoon tomato sauce
- a little less than $1/2$ cup water

Rub the flour, sugar, pepper, salt and nutmeg into the steak. Mix the other ingredients and pour over. Let stand for about an hour, then cook, tightly covered, in a moderate oven for 2 hours. Turn the steak once during cooking.

VIENNA STEAK

Judging by her recipes, my aunt's way with steak was mostly minced. Her book abounds in things like Miss Brett's Aberdeen Sausage – not a "sausage" at all, but more of a steamed meat pudding – and Savoury Mince Hash. Good cooks always bought their piece of steak and minced it themselves. ("You never know what butchers put into their mince, dear.") When I was first married I said to another young wife, repeating my mother's edict – "I never order by phone from the butcher, because I like to look and see what I am getting". My friend said she wouldn't know what to look for, and actually I don't think I did either. But I certainly knew meat was supposed to be looked at. My mother bought her steak and minced it together with an onion, floured it lightly, put it in a pudding basin, with pepper, salt, thyme and a very little water. and let it bob about in a saucepan of boiling water for a long time as if it were a pudding. She opened it up once during the cooking, and gave it a stir. Lacking a pudding basin, I have made it this way in a double boiler. It used to be Kate's favourite dish, until she discovered fried chicken.

But my aunt's Vienna Steak was considered more elegant.

- ♥ 1½ lb. beef steak
- ♥ ¼ cup breadcrumbs
- ♥ 1 egg
- ♥ pepper, salt
- ♥ ½ pint any rough stock
- ♥ 1 teaspoon chopped parsley

My aunt says put your beef through the mincing machine twice, but I now have a butcher I can trust and buy it already minced. I have not had much experience with diamonds, but a good butcher is most certainly a girl's best friend. So, put your minced steak in a basin and add breadcrumbs and seasoning. Bind together with the egg and form it into a roll. Put it into a shallow casserole dish and pour over your rough stock. I use a bouillon cube dissolved in water, of course, but "rough stock" is a nice phrase isn't it? Cover with grease-proof paper and then a lid and cook in a moderate oven for 1½ hours, basting every ¼ hour. Serve with a brown gravy made from the pan juices and flavoured with port or claret, and sprinkled with parsley.

"MY" MEAT LOAF

Vienna steak is a close relative of the meat loaf which I learned to make in New York. It was our friend Ted who taught me my way of doing it, at the time he worked with the insurance company he always referred to as Mother Metropolitan. Mother Metropolitan believed in looking after her employees. She not only offered very cheap turkeys at Christmas by bulk buying for the whole staff (we ate Ted's) but also kept on hand a large supply of umbrellas in case of unexpected rain.

Meat loaf is delicious, cheap and easy to make. As a child, Kate disliked it, loudly, but later on in life when coping with her own budget, she changed her tune. "We had meat loaf for dinner", she wrote, "it's so good, and only costs ..." We live and learn, don't we?

- 1 slice of stale bread 1 inch thick
- 1 cup milk
- 1 lb. ground steak
- 1/2 lb. ground pork
- 1/2 lb. ground veal

- 1 onion
- 1/2 teaspoon finely chopped garlic
- 1/4 cup parsley
- pepper, salt
- 1 teaspoon thyme

Remove crusts from bread. Heat 1/2 cup milk and pour over. Let it stand while you mix the ground meat together. Add onion, garlic and parsley – all finely chopped – pepper, salt and thyme. Add to this the bread and milk mixture and work all together – I find with the hands is the best way. Add the rest of the milk, making a fairly wet mixture and pack it tightly into a loaf tin. Bake in a moderate oven for an hour. No, I didn't forget the egg. Ted and I feel meat loaf is better without. Yes, it does crumble a little when you cut it, but I have never found that any great disadvantage.

MRS GEE'S SAUSAGE CASSEROLE

When my mother spoke of Mrs Gee, I thought she was referring to someone by initial rather than name to prevent my knowing what was going on. I paid rapt attention to a good many dreary adult conversations (while studiously pretending to be wholly occupied with beating eggs or peeling potatoes) before I discovered her name really was Mrs Gee, and no mystery about it at all. It was not until I was quite grown up though that I knew her well enough to ask for and be given this well-loved addition to our kitchen collection.

Build up in your casserole, layers of pork sausages (the plump round ones, not the little thin kind), sliced carrot and sliced onion. Make a sauce in the proportion of:

- ♥ 1 tablespoon sugar
- ♥ 4 tablespoons flour

- ♥ 1 tablespoon each of worcester sauce, tomato sauce, vinegar
- ♥ 1/2 cup sherry

Mix the sugar and flour to a smooth paste with the sauces, vinegar and 1 1/2 cups water, and then stir in the sherry. Pour this over the sausages and vegetables cover and cook very, very slowly for 2 hours, or until the vegetables are very soft. Stir occasionally with a wooden spoon, so it does not stick to the bottom – careful not to break the sausages – and if it seems too thick add a little water. It is better made one day and eaten the next so that if your sausages – shame on the butcher! – exude a lot of fat, you can remove it. Add one extra spoon of sherry, reheat and serve it with apple sauce, mashed potatoes and green peas.

STEAK AND KIDNEY PUDDING

My mother was renowned for her steak and kidney casserole.

I realise now that it is not quite the same as other people's. It is a little simpler and there is more steak and kidneys and less casserole. It was one of the things I always suggested Mother should make when I had a boyfriend coming to dinner. Boyfriends liked my mother's steak and kidney. So did we.

- ♥ 1 large onion
- ♥ 1¹/₂ lb. steak
- ♥ 4 lambs' kidneys
- ♥ flour, pepper and salt

FOR THE CRUST:
- ♥ 3 oz. suet
- ♥ pinch salt
- ♥ 6 oz. flour
- ♥ ¹/₂ teaspoon baking powder

Slice the onion thinly. Cut the steak and kidney into small cubes and dust with flour, pepper and salt. Put this into a basin with a little water. Chop or grate the suet finely and mix it into the salt,

flour and baking powder with your fingers. Add enough water to make a stiff dough. Pat out on a floured board to the size of your bowl and put it on top of your steak and kidney. Mother used an earthenware bowl to cook her casserole in, and tied a floured cloth firmly over the top. I have used one of my mixing bowls with buttered paper tied over it – or of course you can buy proper steam-pudding bowls with lids. Whatever you use the contents should fill about 1 to 2/3 of the bowl before cooking. When you have covered it securely so no water will get in, stand the bowl in boiling water and cook for 2½ hours.

One of my mother's economies was to have in her kitchen a small one-burner kerosene stove for things like this needing long, slow cooking. I often wish I had one too, though somehow these days there seem less of this type of dish. I notice as I write these recipes out for you how often, they say, quite casually, as if there were all the time in the world – simmer 2–3 hours, or even, some of them, put on the back of the stove and allow to cook slowly for 4 or 5 hours. Man in his hasty days no longer has that sort of time to give for "long, slow" anything. A pity, I think.

SPARE RIBS

Funny how recipes get around. The first time I went back to Australia after living in America, I took back a recipe for spare ribs. Some years later, Marjory gave it back to me, as she had adapted it for Australian cooking. This is her version. You may have to cultivate your butcher in order to get the spare ribs, but as I have indicated before, good butchers are worth cultivating.

♥ 3 lb. spare ribs. Cut them into convenient-sized pieces and place in a large baking dish – the sort that has a lid.

Put into a bowl
♥ 4 tablespoons brown sugar
♥ 1 tablespoon prepared mustard

♥ 2 tablespoons worcester sauce
♥ 1/2 cup tomato sauce
♥ 1/2 cup vinegar
♥ 8 oz. tomato purée
♥ 1/4 teaspoon pepper
♥ 2 garlic cloves, chopped
♥ 1 teaspoon paprika
♥ chilli powder to taste
♥ 1/2 teaspoon salt

Mix all this together with 1 cup of water and pour over the spare ribs. Put the lid on your baking dish and bake in a moderate oven for 2 to 3 hours, basting two or three times during cooking. Supply your guests with plenty of paper napkins because fingers are more necessary than forks with spare ribs.

DEVILLED MEAT

One of the big problems for cooks used to be what to do with cold meat. On Sunday you cooked a large joint. Monday you ate it cold. Tuesday, and maybe Wednesday too, you turned it into something else, and Thursday you made soup (or at least that "rough stock") with the bones. But Tuesday and Wednesday were what taxed the ingenuity. One of the tricks was to make lots of gravy on Sunday so at least you had that to help you. But what to do with it. Curry? Rissoles? Shepherd's Pie? Devilled meat perhaps.

- ♥ 1 teaspoon mustard
- ♥ 2 teaspoons vinegar
- ♥ 1/2 oz. butter, melted
- ♥ 1 teaspoon each curry powder, worcester sauce and lemon juice
- ♥ 1/4 cup gravy – you can now get this out of a packet if you haven't been forethoughted about it

Mix the mustard and a little of the vinegar smoothly, and gradually stir in the melted butter, curry powder, worcester sauce, lemon juice and remaining vinegar. Mix well together, then add gravy.

Take slices of meat – it is best if it is rather underdone – and lay them in an oven-proof dish. Pour the mixture over, cover and cook in a hot oven for 10 minutes. Serve with mashed potatoes.

DICK'S CURRY

Curry was another thing we had towards the end of the week when there was a bit of cold meat to be used up. It was in the making of this that my mother was always seduced into throwing together a few fried onion sandwiches and sitting down at the kitchen table to eat them. My brother would join her, because curry was his favourite, and when it was being made he was right there. He and Mother would sit happily consuming the onions which were meant for our dinner while my father and I stood about anxiously asking weren't there going to be any left for the curry? As far as I can remember, they never took any notice of our complaints and in the end, of course, they always had to cook more. Like my father, my brother is a good cook, and, not surprisingly, curry is now his speciality. I don't think he does it quite the way Mother did, for I seem to remember she always cooked hers in a steamer basin bobbing slowly about in a saucepan of boiling water, but the result is just as good. His instructions are certainly as vague as my mother's ever were, but you have to remember that this sort of curry was simply made with what was left over. We always ate our curry with a spoon and fork, which was part of its fascination, and served it with a sweet chutney. It was not mango chutney in those days, though I now think this is best, but of course we didn't have mangoes growing.

Fry 4 large sliced onions in oil until browned but not too crisp.

Cut 1 lb. cold meat (or however much you have) into cubes and brown it with the onions. Add 1 dessertspoon of good dry curry powder and continue to fry a little longer, stirring as you do so. You can use whatever meat you have, beef, mutton, chicken, pork or a mixture. Add sufficient stock to almost cover it, also a tablespoon each of plum jam and coconut, and a handful of sultanas. Let it cook uncovered until it has reduced itself to a thickish consistency. About 10 minutes before you are ready to serve, add some chopped apple and a sliced banana. Taste for seasoning. Depending on how you like it and the strength of your curry powder, you can add chilli powder or cayenne to hot things up a bit. My brother says never add any thickening (certainly not potatoes! What is this, a stew??!) but just let the whole thicken itself as it reduces.

We never used to have pork any way but roasted. Leg or loin, it came with a crispy brown crackling, rich dark gravy and lots of apple sauce. Sometimes, with a loin, my mother stuffed it. She slid her long kitchen knife carefully along between the bone and the meaty part of the chop and then pushed a herb and onion stuffing in with the handle of the wooden spoon. Then she roasted it in the usual way. I had to leave home before I learned there were other things to do with pork.

ELSE'S PORK CHOPS

When Else first came to work in New York she stayed with us in the 52nd Street apartment, sharing a room with bouncy Kate. The Danes were always a hardy race. She and your father went off to work each morning together and came home together each evening. She had only been with us a very little while when he had a birthday. Early in the morning, Kate bounced in to say happy birthday, and having thoroughly woken him up, produced this piece of information. "Mummy and I", she said, "have presents for you, but your Other One didn't know it was your birthday". From that day on Else was known in our household as Daddy's Other One.

- ♥ 3 onions
- ♥ butter and olive oil
- ♥ 1/2 teaspoon chopped garlic (or more if you like)
- ♥ pepper and salt
- ♥ 6 pork chops
- ♥ 3 tomatoes
- ♥ 3 small peppers, green, red and yellow if possible
- ♥ 1/2 teaspoon oregano or basil
- ♥ wine

Slice the onions and cook in butter until they are soft. Add the garlic, pepper, salt and pork chops. If more fat is needed add a little olive oil. Cover and let it cook for 10 minutes, then add the sliced tomatoes, and peppers cut in largish pieces. Add the oregano or basil and correct seasonings. Cook all together until the chops are tender and the sauce a pleasant and colourful mush. If it gets too thick a mush, thin it with a little wine. Serve with rice.

HUGUETTE'S PORK FILLET

Huguette, who lives at the top of one of the lovely old houses that cluster around the Cathedral of St Pierre in Geneva, maintains she cannot cook, but this is obviously nonsense. There are people who walk into a kitchen with familiarity and move about it with naturalness. Huguette is one such. Of course she has known my kitchen for longer than I have, but just the same, a good cook is unmistakable, particularly when she passes out recipes like this.

Take a good-sized pork fillet and paint it generously with Dijon mustard. Pepper and salt it, and wrap it round with rashers of bacon. Then wrap the whole thing in aluminium foil, sit it in a shallow dish and bake for 3/4 hour in a moderate oven. Open the foil – careful not to spill the juice – and allow it to bake another 15 minutes to brown the top. Serve it on a dish surrounded by small sautéed potatoes and mushrooms. Make a gravy with the pan juices, sour cream and a little lemon juice. Mushrooms go well too.

Nowadays rabbit is not perhaps quite such a cheap dish as it used to be when I was young. In those days it really was infinitely cheaper than chicken and – we were always being told – just as good. Actually, I have always liked rabbit so I didn't quarrel with this, and grew up rather expecting that dishes which called for chicken would be made with rabbit. We often had them baked, wrapped round with bacon and stuffed with an onion stuffing. Looking at them now, I wonder how one baked rabbit could have fed us all, but it did. Perhaps they were bigger in those days. We also had them in pies. My aunt made the best one.

AUNT'S RABBIT PIE

Her recipe calls for "2 young rabbits" and I can see her now trotting sturdily off to the market, walking up and down between the stalls, looking a long time before she actually decided what to buy. She wanted to be very sure that her two rabbits really were "young". Nowadays I usually use one rabbit, and probably not as young as my aunt would have liked. However, to make her pie, you need

- 2 young rabbits
- pepper and salt
- 1 thick rasher of bacon
- 1/2 small bay leaf
- 6 peppercorns
- 2 tablespoons butter
- 2 tablespoons lemon juice
- 1/2 oz. flour
- 1/2 pint stock (I use chicken stock)
- 6 very small onions
- 8 mushrooms
- short crust pastry
- 1 egg
- 2 tablespoons milk

You can see that my aunt was a very precise person. I am not so careful with the counting of those bay leaves, peppercorns and mushrooms, but I give you the recipe just as she gave it to me. Cut up the rabbit and dust generously with pepper and salt. Cut up the bacon rasher and fry for a few minutes then set aside. Put the rabbit into a pan with the bay leaf, peppercorns and butter. Cook slowly until the butter has melted, then let the meat cook until it is a pale colour, but not brown. Turn the pieces so that all sides come in contact with the butter. Stir the lemon juice and flour together and stir into the pot with the butter and rabbit. Then add the stock and bring slowly to the boil. Drop into it the whole onions and mushrooms and simmer it moderately fast (this seems to me rather a contradiction in terms, but that's what she said) for 20 minutes. Remove the mushrooms, and allow the rest to simmer for a further 15 minutes or until done, then allow to cool. Take the meat off the bones and put it into a deep pie dish, together with the bacon, onions and mushrooms. Boil the remaining liquid until it has reduced and thickened a little, then strain over the meat in the pie dish. You don't want it too wet. My mother sliced hard boiled eggs on top at this stage but Aunt thought this was gilding the lily. Cover with short crust, beat together the egg and milk and brush all over the pastry. Make a hole in the centre with a knife to let the steam escape and bake in a moderate oven until the crust is brown.

MOTHER'S JELLIED RABBIT

My mother was the one who jellied rabbit, and I loved it this way, too. I have a sneaking suspicion it was one of those recipes where "underground chicken" was used instead of the real thing, but if so, I never knew it.

Cut the rabbit and put it into a pan with sufficient salted water to cover, a small onion, 1 sliced carrot, some parsley, a bay leaf, a little lemon peel and a blade of mace. As far as my mother was concerned, rabbit was always cooked with a blade of mace. Stew quietly until the rabbit is tender and then let it cool in the broth. Take out and cut the meat from the bones. Strain the broth and if necessary add enough water to bring it up to ¾ pint. Taste for seasoning. If you have more than ¾ pint, which you shouldn't, use ½ cup of it to dissolve 3 teaspoons of gelatine. Otherwise dissolve it in hot water, and stir into the strained broth. Slice a hard boiled egg and put it in the bottom of a basin, together with a sprig of parsley and a slice or two of the carrot from the broth. This will be your decoration when the bowl is inverted so arrange it nicely. Then put the rabbit meat on top, and carefully pour over enough broth just to cover. If you have more liquid than you need, set the extra amount in a small cup or bowl and you can cut it up and use it as garnish later on. When the rabbit is set, turn it out, and surround it with pieces of tomato, cucumber, hard boiled egg or that chopped up aspic.

AUDREY'S RABBIT GOOSE

Rabbit in most kitchens masqueraded as chicken frequently, but my sister-in-law is the only one I know who uses it as mock goose. I am not sure it tastes goose, but it certainly tastes good, and though it goes along with family tradition by being slightly vague in spots, I am sure you will manage.

Cut up and soak rabbit in salt and water for 1 hour, then drain, dry and put into a casserole dish. Add a seasoning made from breadcrumbs, herbs, onions, pepper and salt and one chopped apple. Top with grated cheese and pour over all 1/2 cup of milk. Cook slowly for 2 1/2 hours.

MOTHER'S WAY WITH CHICKEN

As I have said, I have nothing against rabbit. I like it. But it isn't chicken. Chicken is not expensive now, but in my childhood it was a treat reserved for birthdays and special occasions. As far as I am concerned, there is still only one way to roast it and that's my mother's way. Chickens were bigger then, and were carved at the table into slices, rather than cut into joints the way the smaller ones are now. It seems to me they had more taste but, on the other hand, they were also frequently tough. Sometimes those "chickens" had no right to the name at all. My aunt, a practical woman as well as one who called a spade a spade writes flatly – "To Cook an Old Fowl. Put 1/2 lb. dripping, and 1 pint of water into a large saucepan and bring it to the boil. Put fowl in on its back and simmer for 2 1/2 hours, then bake in oven for half an hour". That ought to reduce any old fowl to submission, I'd imagine.

We did sometimes have it just plain boiled, with a white sauce full of chopped egg or parsley. But that was when it came openly as "Boiling Fowl" and not masquerading as chicken. Usually though, we had them roasted. It was the stuffing that made my mother's roast chicken different from others and this is how she did it.

To 1 cup of fine white breadcrumbs, add ¼ cup of chopped parsley and a whole, thin slice of lemon chopped as finely as you can chop it. Pepper and salt according to your taste, but it likes a good deal of pepper. Black and freshly ground of course.

Fill half this mixture loosely into your chicken, then put in a nut of butter (a small walnut I'd say) and finally the rest of the crumb mixture. "Close the door" with the chicken liver. I always mistrust chickens which come without livers, but it does happen sometimes and then there's nothing you can do about this last instruction. It won't make too much difference, though the liver adds moisture and flavour. Pepper, salt and paprika the chicken and roast it, basting with butter and seeing that some of that butter dribbles into the stuffing from time to time. When it is tender, put it on a dish and keep it warm while you make the gravy. Mix a little flour with the drippings in the pan and stir in chicken stock, and a grating of lemon peel.

Once when I was staying with my mother, when she was old and ill and supposedly uninterested in food, I made this roast chicken for her and, thinking to improve it, added a little chopped onion to the stuffing. My mother ate what I had given her without comment, but when she had put down her knife and fork, she remarked severely: "Lemon is for chicken. Onion's for duck". I have never done it since.

GINGER CHICKEN

Dutch Hans offered to make this for us — remember? — one snowy Christmas in the mountains of Switzerland. But by the time he came in from skiing, the shops were shut and we had no ginger, and even he couldn't manage without that. He did tell me how to make it though.

Cut up the chicken and rub it well with salt and curry powder. Brown it in a little butter. Add $1/4$ cup of raisins, previously soaked in hot water, 1 tablespoon of chopped stem ginger, 1 tart cooking apple, peeled and chopped, and $1/2$ cup of chicken stock. Cover and let it simmer until the chicken is tender. Taste for seasoning. It may need more salt. I have found that a dash of soy sauce is good, and a little plain yoghurt mixed into the juices does not go amiss. You can add more ginger if you like. Just before serving, add 2 teaspoons of lemon juice and a handful of chopped, blanched almonds. Serve with rice and a salad.

Like many other good Dutch recipes, I feel this has East Indian ancestry, or perhaps it is just that, through their spicier years, the Dutch have acquired such a liking for ginger they pop it in wherever they can. Squares of cheese and stem ginger speared together with toothpicks are also something I learned about in Holland. You serve them with the drinks.

BISHOP'S CHICKEN

Chicken is such a versatile creature. I suppose everybody has their way with it. This one has rather an ecumenical flavour, for it was given to me in Protestant Geneva, by a Dutch Reformed friend who assures me it is what the bishops in Rome do when they have unexpected visitors for lunch. I am not at all sure about this last, but it is a nice touch anyway, and certainly an easy last-minute dish to prepare.

Cut up a cold cooked chicken. You can buy this at the delicatessen, but I don't think too much barbecue sauce improves the flavour. Put a tablespoon of oil in the bottom of a casserole dish and fry the chicken for a moment or two. You will need a little more than a tablespoon if it is a big chicken. Add a piece of lemon peel (oh dear, you don't have to measure it, but about the length of your lemon and half an inch wide – no white pith, please), 8 black olives (more or less, depending on your taste) and a cup of dry white wine. Let it simmer very slowly, covered, for 20 minutes. Just before serving add a tablespoon of brandy and taste for seasoning. Hardly any is necessary, but taste anyway.

PART FOUR
eggs, cheese and salads

THERE WERE MEAT DISHES IN OUR
HOUSE WHEN I GREW UP, AND
MANY CAKES, BUT EGG DISHES,
CHEESE AND SALADS WERE NOT
AS FORTHCOMING. THIS SECTION
CONTAINS THOSE RECIPES I FOUND
ALONG THE WAY – BOTH IN AUSTRALIA
WHERE EVERYONE SEEMED TO HAVE
A QUICHE LORRAINE RECIPE WHEN I
WAS GROWING UP, AND AROUND THE
WORLD WHERE I PICKED UP SOME
NEW FAVOURITES.

♥ ♥

PHIL'S OMELETTE

Prone as I am to forget the names of the boys who figured in my youthful romances, I do remember this one. It is rather unfair really that his name should be attached to this recipe for it was certainly not he who cooked it or gave it to me. I remember his mother as an excellent cook, but this is the only thing I have to show for it. It has little connection with the classical French omelette, but if you forget the misnomer, it is an excellent lunch or light supper dish.

- ♥ 3 eggs
- ♥ 1 slice of white bread ½ inch thick
- ♥ milk
- ♥ 1 teaspoon worcester sauce
- ♥ parsley
- ♥ pepper and salt

Separate eggs and beat yolks with pepper, salt and worcester sauce. Remove the crusts from the bread and pour over enough hot milk to mash it up like bread sauce. Add this to the egg yolks and mix together with the chopped parsley. Beat whites stiffly and fold into the yolk mixture. Fry in butter like small pancakes, turning once.

♥ ♥ ♥ ♥ ♥ ♥ ♥ ♥ ♥ ♥ ♥ ♥ ♥ ♥ ♥ ♥ ♥ ♥ ♥ ♥

SANDWICH SOUFFLÉ

Another egg and bread type recipe is one that I remember making during the war when I was first married. I don't know where I found it, but it is certainly worth keeping.

- ♥ 8 slices of bread
- ♥ 4 oz. butter
- ♥ cheese
- ♥ 1 pint scalded milk
- ♥ ½ teaspoon mustard
- ♥ 1 egg
- ♥ salt

Make small sandwiches of the bread, butter and cheese, cutting off all crusts, and topping each sandwich with a little extra butter and a slice of cheese. Place them in a buttered pie dish. Mix the mustard with a little milk. Beat the egg, add the milk and salt, and then the mustard. Pour over the sandwiches, and allow to stand for at least an hour. Stand dish in a larger one of hot water and bake in a moderate oven for ½ hour or until golden brown.

CRABMEAT SOUFFLÉ

A fancier version of the above is made with fish instead of cheese.
I always use crabmeat, but there's no rule against experimenting.

- ♥ 1 can crabmeat (7 or 8 oz.)
- ♥ 8 slices bread
- ♥ 1/2 cup finely chopped celery
- ♥ 3 spring onions, chopped
- ♥ parsley
- ♥ mayonnaise
- ♥ 2 teaspoons Dijon mustard
- ♥ 1 egg
- ♥ 2 cups scalded milk
- ♥ salt and cayenne pepper
- ♥ cheese

Drain the crabmeat and remove the tendons and any pieces of
shell. Mix it with the celery, spring onions (chop some of the green
as well as the white part), parsley, mustard, cayenne pepper and
enough mayonnaise to bind it. Taste for salt. You may not need
any. Make the sandwiches with this filling. Cut them in quarters,
and place a slice of cheese on top of each. Put them in a buttered
oven-proof dish. Beat the egg and add the milk, pepper and salt.
Pour over the sandwiches and let stand for at least 1/2 hour. Stand
the dish in another of hot water and bake in a medium oven for
1/2 hour or until set and brown on top. Serve with a green salad.

REG'S QUICHE LORRAINE

Despite its French title, this came to me in Australia. It was given to me by a very good old friend who had always been knowledgeable and interested in good food, but who, after his wife's death, also became interested in cooking. He was always very modest about his efforts, but the recipes he gave me are all excellent and will keep his memory in my house and kitchen for many years to come.

FOR THE PASTRY:
- ♥ 4 oz. butter
- ♥ 4 oz. package cream cheese
- ♥ 1 cup plain flour

Cream butter and cheese together and beat thoroughly. Add flour and blend with a fork. Wrap in waxed paper and refrigerate for about 1 hour. Roll out to fit in 8 or 9 inch pie plate.

FOR THE FILLING:
- ♥ 8 oz. sliced Swiss cheese
- ♥ 6 rashers of bacon, grilled
- ♥ 3 large or 4 medium eggs
- ♥ 1 teaspoon onion juice or 1 teaspoon grated onion
- ♥ 1/2 pint cream
- ♥ 1/2 level teaspoon nutmeg
- ♥ 1/2 level teaspoon salt
- ♥ sprinkle of pepper

Cut cheese into 1 inch strips. Crumble grilled and well-drained bacon. Beat eggs lightly with onion, cream and seasonings. Pour over bacon and cheese in pastry shell and bake in preheated 425°F oven for 10 minutes, then lower heat to 300°F for 25 minutes or more, until a silver knife comes out clean.

BISHOP'S DELIGHT

In a roundabout way, this really did come from a bishop – or at least from his kitchen. It is one of those recipes – of which I have several – which taste better than they sound. Don't turn up your nose and say, "Cold scrambled eggs? With cream?" Just make it and serve it, and you will find, as I have, that it's one of the most useful summer dishes there is.

- ♥ 6 eggs
- ♥ 6 dessertspoons milk
- ♥ butter, pepper and salt

Scramble the eggs with the milk, butter, pepper and salt in a gentle, creamy fashion and put them in an even layer in a flat serving dish. Whip 1/2 cup of heavy cream and – when the eggs are quite cold of course – spread it over the top. Cover this with thin slices of ham, and some sliced stuffed olives, and over the top pour – very gently so as not to disturb the cream – 1/2 cup of liquid, but cold, aspic. Put in the refrigerator until the aspic is set and serve with a salad. You may find that you will have to vary these proportions according to your dish, the number of your guests and the size of their appetites. For your guidance, the egg should be about 1 1/2 to 2 inch deep, the cream a little less than 1/2 inch and the aspic just a thin film over the top.

This brings me to the subject of aspic. In most places, aspic powder can be bought in tins, or you can set clear chicken stock or bouillon with a little gelatine. In either case, you can use your imagination and add to these a little brandy, a little sherry, a little lemon juice. Any of these are possible ...

However, I feel I must tell you that making aspic in the more or less traditional way is one of the most satisfying things I know. I do not wish to be told the technical reasons why it does what it does. It is one of those miracles that occur in kitchens, and it delights me. I make it this way.

Put 4 cups of strong chicken broth, cold and free from fat, into a saucepan, not an aluminium one, with 1 teaspoon tomato paste and 9 level teaspoons of gelatine. (If you buy your gelatine in those little measured envelopes, this is the equivalent of 3 of them. If your stock is so good that it jellies of its own accord use less gelatine.) Add to the saucepan 3 egg whites which you have first beaten to soft peaks. Put the pan on the fire and continue to beat with a little wire whisk until it comes to a rolling boil. Take off the fire and allow to stand without touching it for 10 minutes. After that pour it into a bowl through a cloth which has been wrung out in iced water. Look what has happened! Out of that murky looking mess you started off with, you have brought forth clear, sparkling aspic. Don't ask how or why. Accept the miracle and give thanks. I love making aspic.

MADAME BOSSARD'S FONDUE

Well you can't live in Switzerland without learning how to make fondue, can you? This particular recipe was given me in exchange for a little English conversation. It is the one I always use.

Allow 1 glass of white wine and
3/4 cup gruyére cheese per person

Rub around your casserole with a cut clove of garlic, then put a little very finely chopped garlic into it. The fondue casserole in Switzerland is called a caquelon. It is usually glazed earthenware, round, squat and with a short stubby handle. Grate the cheese.

Take 1/2 teaspoon of flour per person and mix smoothly in a little kirsch. Warm the wine in the casserole, with the chopped garlic, and as it begins to heat, add the cheese, stirring all the time. Also a little ground black pepper. When it is melted add the flour and kirsch mixture, and go on stirring.

Take quickly to the table and place on a methylated spirit burner, with the flame adjusted so that the fondue continues to simmer.

While you have been doing all this, your guests have been sitting at the table occupying themselves by breaking up their bread into bite-sized pieces and enjoying the delicious smell which is coming from the kitchen. By the time you come in with your steaming casserole, they will helpfully have lighted the burner for you so there is no delay. Then they will take their long forks, with a piece of bread firmly fixed on it, and plunge it into the fondue, stirring then eating. A little more pepper perhaps? But mind you don't burn your mouth. Mangez, et bon appetit.

Of course there are some we know who use a full cup of cheese per person, who add a little nutmeg to the mixture, or an extra glass of kirsch at the end. All these are permissible. The recipe I have given here is just as it was given to me. Drink white wine with it. A glass of kirsch taken at the end helps the digestion, and never, never, never, serve ice cream as dessert. A little fresh fruit salad, if you must, but anything very cold is a disaster.

And one last word. When you and your guests have stirred and eaten until only a film of fondue is left on the bottom, wait a little and let it cook until it is crisp and brown. Then take a knife and lift it – carefully, carefully – off the casserole, a thin toasted cheese pancake – and divide it up. That is the religieuse. Delicious!

VAL'S PASTICCIO

If you have a cold winter's night and a lot of mouths to feed, this is the answer. It is excellent for buffet suppers and can be made the night before and reheated. Depending on appetites, it serves approximately 12 people, as it stands, so for family or small dinner party consumption, halve it.

Boil about 3/4 lb. of macaroni. Do not overcook. Strain, and return to the pan with plenty of butter and, when it has cooled a little, add 3 unbeaten egg whites, and a cup of grated cheese.

Meanwhile, fry a good cup of chopped onions in butter, add 2 lb. chopped beef and stir until crumbly. Then add 1/2 cup or so of tomato purée, 1 glass wine and liquid as necessary. Also salt and pepper. Cook, covered, for some 40 minutes, watching that your meat ends up a thickish paste and not a runny sauce. Add 1/2 cup of soft breadcrumbs.

Butter a baking dish. Put in the macaroni, and spread the meat on top of it. Make a very thick bechamel sauce with 3 cups of milk, 1 cup of flour, 3 tablespoons butter, 1/2 teaspoon nutmeg, salt and pepper. To this add 3 unbeaten eggs yolks and 1/3 cup grated cheese. Spread this sauce over the meat, and sprinkle with grated cheese. Pour a little melted butter over the top and bake for 45 minutes in a hot oven.

BASIL'S MACARONI CHEESE

My mother made macaroni cheese, like many a good Australian cook before and since, by making a nice rich cheese sauce, putting cooked macaroni into it, topping it with more cheese and baking it to a crispy brown. She did the same thing with cauliflower, and very good they both were. But Basil's dish is different, and since prising the recipe out of him, a good many years ago now, I have never gone back to making it the old way. To do it properly does entail having garlic growing in your garden, as you will see, which is a slight problem. If you are a flat dweller, who doesn't care to grow garlic in your window box, then you must do as I have been forced to do – use chopped green onion tops, and add the veriest touch of garlic powder.

One small cup of macaroni, cooked in boiling water, salt and a little oil (to prevent it clinging together) until soft. Drain, wash well and drain again.

In a large bowl, beat one egg and add a good cup of milk, 1/4 teaspoon cayenne pepper, a few shakes of really hot pepper sauce, and 1/2 teaspoon salt. Take 2 fine garlic leaves (here we go, you see) and cut them up with scissors. Add them to the egg and milk together with 1 cup of grated cheese. Mix this well with the macaroni, and put into a buttered round casserole. Cover with a LOT of breadcrumbs, then grated cheese and dobs of butter.

Stand in another dish of hot water, and cook in a moderate oven for just over 3/4 hour.

MACARONI AND MUSHROOMS

And here's an American version. It comes from that little kitchen on 74th Street, presided over by our good friend Bill.

- ♥ 1/2 lb. elbow macaroni
- ♥ 1/2 lb. sharp cheddar cheese
- ♥ 1/2 lb. mushrooms
- ♥ milk
- ♥ breadcrumbs
- ♥ grated parmesan

Put the macaroni into boiling salted water and cook it for 2 or 3 minutes after it resumes boiling. A little cooking oil in the water prevents it sticking together, otherwise rinse. Cut the cheese into small cubes or in slices at least 1/4 inch thick. Cut the mushrooms in similar slices. Fresh mushrooms are better but tinned may be used. In a buttered casserole, arrange layers of macaroni, mushrooms and cheese in that order, ending with cheese. Add milk to half cover. Top with breadcrumbs and grated parmesan, and dot with butter. Cover and bake at 350°F for approximately 1/2 hour until milk is absorbed and cheese melted. Uncover, and increase heat to 400°. Bake for 15 minutes or until lightly browned.

FOUR SALADS

Yes of course we had salads when we were young. The garden
provided us with lettuce, cucumber, tomatoes and beetroot, so what
more could you ask? A lot, I'm afraid. I grew up hating salads. Or
perhaps not so much hating them, as thinking them a great and
terrible bore. And why shouldn't I indeed. My family did terrible things
to all those garden-fresh goodies, and I am sure we were not alone
in this. Everybody I knew did the same thing. We cut everything up
very fine, and either soaked it in vinegar (ugh!) or produced a slightly
sweet, salad cream, boiled, or made (I am not joking – it's nothing to
joke about) with sweetened condensed milk. It wasn't until I went to
Sydney to live that I – very tentatively at first – tasted a good green
salad with a simple oil and vinegar dressing. It was our dear Donnie,
who guided Kate's first tottering steps and looked after us all so
well until we went to America, who introduced me to it. Her way of
doing it was simply to combine lettuce (not shredded), with tomato
(in wedges rather than fine slices) and cucumber. She salted it, and
poured over 3 tablespoons of oil to 1 of vinegar. She used the pepper
grinder last. I very quickly learned that this was far removed from the
ones I knew, and over the years have discovered that there are others
I can eat and enjoy. I offer you four.

BILL'S CAESAR SALAD

Caesar salad is such a classic that perhaps I should not include it
here, but it is my favourite and I feel it should have a place in your
kitchen heritage. It was Bill again, who taught me how to make it.
And it was this I asked for when we returned to New York after a
two-year absence and Bill and Ruth phoned us in London to say, "We
expect you for dinner the night you arrive, what do you want to eat?"

I think you will find that Bill's version is slightly different from the traditional one.

Cut sliced bread into small crustless cubes – enough to make 1/2 cup. Cook these croutons quickly in oil with 1/2 clove of garlic in it, until they are lightly browned and crisp. Drain on paper towel, salting them a little while still hot and set them aside.

Use mixed greens for contrast in texture, colour and taste – romaine, chicory, escarole, iceburg or Boston lettuce – whatever is available where you are. Bill says "the equivalent of 3 bunches", which is difficult to translate, but since this recipe is for six people, what you do is to take enough greens for that number. Wash, dry them thoroughly and tear into bite-sized pieces. Never use a knife on a lettuce.

Rub a large wooden salad bowl with a cut clove of garlic. Your bowl must be big enough to allow for the tossing later on. Finely chop 1/4 garlic clove and put it in the bowl. Add to it:

- 1 1/2 tablespoons vinegar (preferably French)
- 3 1/2 tablespoons olive oil (Italian or Greek)
- 1 teaspoon dry mustard
- a dash of worcester sauce or Tabasco

Mix this together. Drain 1 can of anchovy fillets, chop or mash and add to the bowl. On top of this put your greens, also

- 1 tablespoon grated parmesan cheese
- 1/3 lb. roquefort or blue cheese, coarsely crumbled

Toss well. Break over it 1 egg, coddled for 1 minute. Add the croutons. Mix again, and serve.

NORMA'S RICE AND TUNA SALAD

This salad always brings back the smell of chops on a barbecue, the vision of laden tables on a long cool verandah, and the laughter of friends. It was only one of several salad recipes I collected that day, but it is the one I have used most often.

- ♥ 2/3 cup uncooked rice – cook and strain
- ♥ 1/2 cup mayonnaise
- ♥ 1/4 cup chutney
- ♥ 3 tins tuna fish (7 oz.)
- ♥ almonds – not peeled, but coarsely cut and toasted
- ♥ 1/2 teaspoon salt
- ♥ 1 cup diagonally cut celery
- ♥ 2 teaspoons curry powder
- ♥ 1 medium tin pineapple chunks (drained)

Mix mayonnaise, chutney, curry powder and salt. Add rice, pineapple, celery and tuna. Mix carefully, cover and chill. Before serving add the almonds.

TABOOLI

In the days when our wanderings took us fairly frequently through Beirut, I acquired a liking for Tabooli. Quite recently, a Lebanese girl coming through Geneva showed me how to make it. She stood in my little kitchen and chopped and sliced and tasted – throwing in a little of this and a handful of that – with all a good cook's disregard for actual quantities. I think perhaps it doesn't matter with Tabooli, but for your sake I have tried to reduce Marcelle's airy chatter as she worked, into some semblance of a recipe.

"My mother makes the best Tabooli", Marcelle said, "and this is how she does it. You take a lot of parsley".

A lot of parsley is hard to measure. Marcelle bought it from the street market in the Place des Alpes, where the summer stalls are piled high with such delights that if I were not an Australian I would immediately become a vegetarian. She tipped her fresh parsley out onto my yellow table top, in a bright cascade of curly green. "We'll need all that", she said. "Will you chop it please."

So I chopped. I went on chopping for quite sometime. And I finished with 2 cups of chopped parsley. "Not too fine", said Marcelle, "or it spoils the flavour".

Meanwhile she took ½ cup of cracked wheat, and soaked it in enough cold water to cover. This is the ingredient you may find difficult to get, but there are not many cities these days which do not have a Greek or Lebanese store tucked away somewhere if you really look. "Let it soak about 15 minutes", she said. "Some people leave it longer, but my mother says that's enough. Then squeeze it out, very thoroughly with your hands." Meanwhile, Marcelle chopped four spring onions, green as well as white parts, a little fresh mint (about one sprig) and 1 large tomato. Also one small brown onion. She chopped this very fine, then put salt on it, and squeezed it out a little in a paper towel to get some of the juice out. "That's my mother's trick", she said.

After this, all was mixed together, and over the top went about one tablespoon of fresh lemon juice, three of vegetable oil, pepper and salt. A great deal of tasting went on here, and maybe a little more lemon juice was added. Finally, on top for decoration went another small tomato chopped coarsely. The whole was put into the refrigerator to get it really cold.

It is delicious any way, but I like it best with shish kebab or roast lamb.

"MY" POTATO SALAD

When we first went to the United States and lived in that little white clapboard house in Larchmont, I had the incredible luck to find myself right next door to someone who loved cooking quite as much as I do. You will remember the great cooking orgies – what Jean-Daniel later referred to as "les crises de cuisine" – that went on between us, particularly I think the day that we both, slavishly and enthusiastically following TV instructions, made cookies with coffee grounds in them. Two tired husbands walking back from the commuter train sniffed the good kitchen smells and said, "Ah, cookies!" Then they tasted them. Oh dear, what a fuss! But mostly, we did alright, and we certainly had fun. It is strange that out of all that cooking, this really is the only thing I have brought with me – except memories. It is the way Dorothy showed me, and I have made it ever since.

- ♥ 4 good sized potatoes, boiled and skinned
- ♥ 1 carrot
- ♥ 2 hard boiled eggs
- ♥ parsley, chives, pepper, salt
- ♥ mayonnaise

Cut the potatoes in cubes. Grate the carrot. Chop the eggs coarsely, and the parsley and chives finely. Actually "chop" is the wrong word for chives, because I believe they should be cut with the kitchen scissors. It is better for them. Mix all this together, salt it and pepper generously. Coarsely ground black pepper is best. Then add enough mayonnaise to make a good creamy consistency. I like a lot of mayonnaise, and the salad itself likes to sit and get acquainted for a while before you use it.

"MY" SALAD DRESSING

This is only "my" salad dressing in the sense that it is the one I always make. The recipe was given to me by Dione Lucas one snowy morning in New York, and if you are lucky enough to have one of her cookbooks, you may well find it there. However, she was a great one for changing recipes according to her mood, so if your printed version isn't quite the same, don't worry. This is exactly the way she told it to me, sitting on the stools in the pretty kitchen of her brownstone house in East 60th Street, looking out on the little church of All Saints. It is the best one I know.

Take a screwtop jar and in the bottom put

- 1 teaspoon of salt
- 1 heaped teaspoon freshly cracked black and white pepper
- 1/4 teaspoon granulated sugar
- 1/2 level teaspoon dry mustard
- 1 teaspoon Dijon mustard
- 1 teaspoon lemon juice
- 1/2 teaspoon very finely chopped garlic
- 3 tablespoons good tarragon vinegar
- 3 tablespoons olive oil
- 9 tablespoons vegetable oil
- 1 raw egg

Shake all well together. It will keep in the refrigerator for one week or more.

Dione didn't believe in rutting garlic through a garlic press, but preferred to put a little salt on it and chop it finely with a knife. I must admit I have sometimes, when in a hurry, used the press, but it is better the other way. I have also sometimes varied the proportion of the oils because I like olive oil. Dione always used French olive oil.

If, by chance, you want a vinaigrette sauce, you can start off in exactly the same way, but after you have shaken it well add

- 1 tablespoon finely chopped fresh shallots and an extra 1/2 teaspoon garlic, chopped
- 2 tablespoons finely chopped fresh parsley
- 1 tablespoon finely chopped fresh tarragon
- 1 tablespoon chopped chives
- 1 finely chopped hard boiled egg

That same morning Dione also told me how she made tarragon vinegar. Of course, I do realise that you'll probably buy yours ready-made, but maybe one day ...

In a gallon jar, stuff as many tarragon leaves and stalks as possible. Fill the jar up with good cider vinegar and keep it in a dark place for 3 months. As you use it, add more vinegar.

PART FIVE
afters

IN MY CHILDHOOD, "AFTERS" WERE
FIRMLY DIVIDED INTO THREE – BAKED,
BOILED AND COLD. I DON'T THINK WE
EVER REFERRED TO THEM AS DESSERTS
– CERTAINLY NOT AS THE MORE REFINED
"SWEETS", A TERM OF WHICH MY
MOTHER THOROUGHLY DISAPPROVED.
BAKED, BOILED, OR COLD, IT WAS
ALWAYS JUST "PUDDING". "WHAT'S
FOR PUDDING?" WE ASKED. AND AS I
WRITE THAT QUESTION ANOTHER ONE
SPRINGS TO MIND.

♥ ♥

AS THE GIRL OF THE FAMILY, IT WAS ALWAYS MY JOB TO LAY THE TABLE, AND EACH DAY AS I SET OUT TO DO THIS, I WOULD ASK "WHAT'S FOR DINNER?" And my mother would reply, "Knives and forks, spoons and forks and fruit plates and knives". It is only right this minute that it has struck me as being a funny answer. Though I'd have been fairly put out if I had asked, "What's for pudding?" and been told "spoons and forks". That was a serious question and all important. If you didn't eat your first course you didn't get any pudding, so it was just as well to know ahead of time whether the "afters" were worth it. Actually, in a way, you had a pretty fair idea of what was coming, for if the first course was baked you got a baked pudding. Otherwise it was probably boiled. The day after a roast dinner there was apt to be a cold baked pudding. The economy of our kitchen was that if you had the oven going, you baked as much in it as you possibly could. My mother obviously was not working with the sort of oven I have had to cope with so often when, if you managed to get in a small roast, there certainly was not any room for anything else. You only got cold gelatine-type puddings in the summer. And we never had ice cream. That was not considered a pudding, but something you bought in a cone and licked, preferably outdoors with the sun warm upon your back. That is still the most satisfactory way to eat it.

♥ ♥

MOTHER'S ROLY POLY

Roly Poly was another favourite and Mother's was the best. Not the cheapest, perhaps, but the best.

FOR THE PASTE:

- ♥ 1 cup flour
- ♥ 1 pinch salt
- ♥ 1 teaspoon baking powder
- ♥ 1 tablespoon butter
- ♥ a little milk

Mix the flour, salt and baking powder together and rub in the butter with your fingertips. Then add enough milk to make a soft dough. Roll out about 1/2 inch thick and spread with jam (or if you prefer, chopped apples). Roll up and place the roll in a pie dish.

FOR THE SYRUP:

- ♥ 1 small cup sugar
- ♥ small 1/2 cup butter
- ♥ 1 large cup water

Heat all together in a saucepan and when melted pour over the Roly Poly. Bake for about 1 hour.

It was of this pudding that Mother told a story. Children were supposed to eat what they were given, but we actually preferred an inside piece of Roly Poly rather than an end, and sometimes we said so. This is the story Mother told us. Three men were about to eat a delicious Roly Poly, and the first to be served said he'd like an inside piece please.

Whereupon the man who was serving said, "That's fine. Me and my mate like the ends". Then he cut the Roly neatly in half, giving half to himself, half to his mate, and none at all to the fussy one.

AUNTIE CHICK'S LEMON PIE

Auntie Chick was my Godmother. I don't know how she acquired that nickname but I suppose it was in the same way that some people get called Dot or Mouse or Scrap. Her real name was Rose. She was married to my mother's Uncle Noel, whom as a child I absolutely adored. He was an inventor, which makes any man fairly endearing to a child, but I am not at all sure what he invented. I do remember he built some very pleasant houses out of old-fashioned tram cars but he surely must have done other things too. After Auntie Chick's death he quarrelled with the rest of the family, and after that nobody was speaking to him, which was all very sad, for he had been such fun and we all loved him so.

Soak 2 oz. breadcrumbs in $1/2$ cup water, and add 1 cup sugar. Beat the yolks of 3 eggs, and add 1 oz. slightly melted butter. Grate the rind of one lemon and add it to the eggs, together with the juice of two lemons. Mix with the breadcrumbs and sugar. Beat all together for 5 minutes. Fill a greased pie dish with the mixture, and bake in a moderate oven for $1/2$ hour. Make a meringue with egg whites when the pudding is cooked, spread this on top and return to the oven to brown slightly. Serve with whipped cream.

BAKED THATCH PUDDING

This used to be my absolute favourite pudding. Each Sunday I hoped we'd have it, and if we did then I hoped Mother would forget and give it to us again the following Sunday. If I were asked what I'd like, Thatch Pudding was always my reply. "But we had it just the other day", my brother would say. That never seemed a legitimate reason for not repeating it. I always did have boarding school tastes, you see.

Mix 3 tablespoons of flour to a cream with a little milk. Beat together the yolks of 2 eggs and a little sugar. Add 3 large cups of boiling milk to the flour mixture and to this add the yolks and sugar. Whip the egg whites to a stiff froth and fold in. Bake for 25 minutes in a moderate oven.

MOTHER'S LEMON PUDDING

For some reason I didn't have this recipe, nor was it anywhere in my mother's book, although she made it often and I liked it. Eventually I found it in my aunt's, labelled "Spot's Lemon Pudding", and that brought back a flood of memories. Both my mother and my aunt were apt to call each other Spot on occasion, and when we children enquired why, they'd laugh and say "Oh that's an old story", and then they'd look at each other and laugh some more. You would hear them in the kitchen working away together, each referring to the other as Spot and their voices so alike you could never tell who was talking to whom. I never did discover what the joke was.

- ♥ 5 oz. soft breadcrumbs
- ♥ 2 oz. sugar
- ♥ 3 oz. butter
- ♥ ½ pint boiling milk
- ♥ 2 eggs
- ♥ rind and juice of 1 lemon

Put the breadcrumbs, sugar and butter into a bowl, and pour over the boiling milk. Cover it with a plate and let stand for half an hour. Beat the eggs, and add, together with the juice and rind of the lemon. Mix well, and bake until set and a little brown on top.

DELICIOUS PUDDING

We never lived in a house without a lemon tree, so perhaps this is the reason for the number of lemon puddings we had. Delicious Pudding is one of the great Australian standbys, I think. I don't know that there is much difference between one recipe and another except that some may be a little more specific about the sugar. This is the one my mother used, and I've decided ½ cup of sugar is sufficient.

- ♥ 1 tablespoon butter
- ♥ ½ to 1 cup of sugar
- ♥ 2 eggs (separated)
- ♥ 2 tablespoons SR flour
- ♥ juice and rind of 1 lemon
- ♥ ½ pint milk

Cream the butter and sugar, add beaten egg yolks and then flour. Add the lemon juice and rind, then milk. Beat the egg whites stiff and fold in. Stand the dish in another of water and cook until set, puffed and brown, about 30–45 minutes. There was also a chocolate version of this, which was made in exactly the same way, but omitting the lemon and using 1 tablespoon of cocoa and a heaped tablespoon of flour.

MOTHER'S APPLE CHARLOTTE

There was always a great deal of discussion in our household about Apple Charlotte. First of all there was a question as to whether what my mother made was Apple Charlotte or Brown Betty. Mother said firmly that Brown Betty had breadcrumbs not bread slices, and I agreed with her. Not that I knew, of course, I simply worked on the assumption that what Mother said in the kitchen was right. (I must admit that I have since seen recipes for Apple Charlotte made with breadcrumbs, and I have a feeling that any real honest-to-goodness Charlotte should be turned out, apple or not. Mother's stayed in its dish and was spooned out sweet, syrupy, brown, crisp and delicious.) The second bone of contention was about flavouring. My father said apples needed cloves and my mother said Apple Charlotte needed lemon, not cloves. My brother said he actually would prefer neither, as, if there was a lemon pip in it he always got it and if there were cloves, well he'd get those too. I simply added another spoonful of cream while my elders weren't looking and ate up.

Peel, core and slice the apples and cook them with a slice of lemon, sugar, a pinch of salt and a very little water. Take the crusts off thin slices of bread and butter them generously. Line a pie dish with this bread and fill it with the apple. Cover the top with more thin slices of buttered bread and sprinkle with a little sugar. Bake for about an hour or until the bread is crisp and brown.

LUISE'S APPLES IN SAUCE

Luise was a friend who came from the country to stay with us just before the war. She has certainly left her imprint in all our kitchens, for I find this recipe not only written in my cookbook, but also in my mother's, my aunt's and my sister-in-law's.

Peel, core and quarter apples and place in a pie dish. Mix 1 small cup of sugar with 1 tablespoon butter and 2 tablespoons of flour. Spread over the apples.

Add 1½ cups of cold water and pour over the apples. Bake in a moderate oven for about 1 hour.

APPLE CRUNCH

This is my addition to the apple harvest and it came from the Rudolph Steiner School in New York. Once when I made it in London, small cousin Ralph, who attended a Steiner school there, took one look at it and said, "Oh we get this at school", so obviously wherever Rudolph Steiner goes, there goes apple crunch also.

- ❤ 4 or 5 apples thinly sliced
- ❤ *1/2 cup sugar
- ❤ 1 teaspoon cinnamon

Place the sliced apples on a glass pie plate, and cover them with mixed sugar and cinnamon. Let them stand for about 1/2 hour until the sugar is dissolved. Then cover with the following batter:

- ❤ *2 tablespoons butter
- ❤ *1/2 cup sugar
- ❤ 1 egg, well beaten
- ❤ *1/2 cup flour, sifted together with
- ❤ 1 teaspoon baking powder and
- ❤ 1/2 teaspoon salt

Cream the butter and sugar well, and add the beaten egg. Cream these together and then add the flour, baking powder and salt. Beat well. Bake in a moderate oven until golden brown, 30–40 minutes.

* American measurements (see page 18)

Although our apple puddings were served with either cream or custard, sour cream has a friendly feeling for all apples. To a cup of sour cream, try adding a tablespoon of sugar, and the grated rind of an orange. You will not be sorry.

OUR HELEN'S APPLE PIE

I wish I had really written down, at the time, the way Our Helen made apple pie, during those years she and I shuffled round the tiny kitchen in New York. It was always Kate's favourite, requested every birthday, and only Helen could make it. The apple pies of my childhood were what the Americans call "Deep Dish". You stew your apples first (complete with clove) and then cover with a good short crust. But Helen's was different and the only kind, as far as Kate was concerned.

Last time we were in New York, Helen said to me, "I must bake an apple pie for Kate while you're here". I said, "That's very kind of you but we're only here a few days, we're staying at a hotel ... maybe next time". "Kate always has my apple pie in New York", Helen said. So Kate had it. Baked in someone else's oven, because Helen herself had no kitchen, and brought to us at a cocktail party the night before we left. "Whatever will you do with it?" I said to Kate, figuring it didn't actually go with cocktails. "I always have Helen's apple pie in New York", she answered, as if that settled that, and cut herself a large slice immediately. She finished it off for breakfast before getting on the plane. Every crumb.

So you see it is impossible to write this book without including Helen's apple pie, although I don't really have the recipe. I've watched her do it a million times though, and I am sure somehow we can manage. But mind you, I don't think any of us will ever make it quite the way Our Helen did.

Line a round pie dish with short crust. Helen always bought packet pastry and made it according to the rules. She rolled it very thinly, using half to line the pie dish and keeping the rest for the top. Into this she sliced her apples. Tart cooking apples peeled and sliced finely and piled higher in the centre of the dish. They sit down a little when cooked.

Over these she sprinkled about $1/2$ cup of sugar, $1/2$ teaspoon cinnamon, a little nutmeg and some grated lemon rind. A dab or two of butter and then on went the top crust, pressed down round the edge with a fork to make a fancy border and pricked a couple of times with the same fork to let the steam out. She also brushed the top with a little milk to brown it.

Then she put the whole into a hot oven, turning it down to medium after 10 minutes. It took about another 30 to 40 minutes for the apples to be soft, the pastry brown and the whole apartment filled with the bonus a good apple pie brings – the sweet unmistakable and enticing smell of apples, spice and crisp warm crust.

A variation given to me by a Czech friend in New York which Helen certainly never used but which I can recommend all the same, is to cover the bottom of the pastry with a thin layer of finely chopped walnuts before putting on the apples.

And the Swiss version of this is, I suppose:

TARTÉ AUX POMMES

I use my own short crust, and roll it not as thinly as Helen did for her apple pie, but maybe ⅛ inch thick. With this, line a round cake tin – or if you have a flan ring, so much the better. It's easier to remove the tarté at the end. Peel and quarter your apples, slice them thinly and arrange on the pastry in an overlapping pattern as neatly and prettily as you can, so that the pastry is well covered and there is plenty of apple. Cook this in a medium oven until the apple is soft and the pastry crisp, about 30 minutes. While it is cooking melt a little quince jelly. When the tarté is cooked and still hot, sprinkle over it 2 tablespoons of sugar, and then paint carefully over the apples – leaving your pattern undisturbed – the melted jelly, to give it a shiny glaze.

You can also make this tarté with prune plums instead of apples. Cut them in half, remove the stones, and make your design with the cut side up. Sprinkle with sugar but omit the jelly.

BAKED FRUIT PUDDING

We had a lot of cakey puddings. Sometimes baked in one of those pie dishes I keep referring to, with a layer of jam in the bottom and sort of plain cake on top. Served hot and with custard. Called, I think, Castle Pudding. Sometimes more or less the same thing was baked in small, tall round tins, and turned out, so that the jam (always red in colour) ran down the sides in hot, sticky rivers. These were called Red Caps. But the one I liked best was the kind that had fruit underneath and cake on top. It was a less solid cake than the others and moister because of the fruit. As far as I know, my mother always used what she called her "One, Two, Three" recipe for the top. It is a very useful formula, and makes excellent small cakes too, if you want them. Of course you have to use your imagination about that milk, but it isn't too difficult.

- ♥ 1 tablespoon butter
- ♥ 2 tablespoons sugar
- ♥ 3 tablespoons SR flour
- ♥ 1 egg
- ♥ a little milk

Cream the butter and sugar, add the egg, then sifted flour and enough milk to make a good batter. I have a feeling it may be necessary – depending on the size of your pie dish – to double the amount for this pudding. If that happened, mother used the largest egg she could find (they didn't come in quite such regular sizes then as they do today), and a little more milk. But you can use 2 eggs if you like. It makes a richer batter.

Fill your dish about ¾ full of hot stewed fruit and spread the batter over the top. You can drop it on from a spoon and let it spread itself as it cooks if that's easier. Bake in a hot oven until the cake tests done. Any kind of stewed fruit can be used. If we had it with apple (as we often did), mother sometimes replaced 1 tablespoon of sugar with 1 of honey, which was good, too.

FANNY'S RHUBARB SOUFFLÉ

Some time before the Second World War, a cousin of my father's, who'd been born and brought up in England, decided to come and visit her Australian relatives. She brought with her a friend called Fanny, who, at some time during the visit, admitted she was interested in cooking. I promptly asked her for a recipe and was bitterly disappointed when she presented me with her Rhubarb Soufflé. Rhubarb (we had masses of it growing) was my most unfavourite dessert. But with the advent of this recipe I discovered there were ways I could eat it and like it. Another way was simply by adding a packet of frozen strawberries to a bowl of stewed rhubarb, but that was many years later, so let's get back to the soufflé.

Fill a pudding dish three parts full of rhubarb, cut up into small pieces and well sugared. Take 6 bananas, not over-ripe, and the whites of 3 eggs. Beat the eggs into a stiff froth, and mash up the bananas with 3 dessertspoons of sugar. Then blend the two well together and pour over the rhubarb. Sprinkle with chopped, blanched almonds, and bake for 20 minutes in a hot oven, calculating the time so as to take the dish straight to the table as it comes out. Serve with thick cream. Enough for six people.

BOILED STEAMED APPLE PUDDING

Mother made a steamed apple pudding too, which I liked. Also without cloves – but I don't ever remember there being the same discussion over this one as with the Apple Charlotte.

- ♥ 1 oz. butter
- ♥ 1 small cup sugar
- ♥ 1 egg
- ♥ 1 small cup milk
- ♥ 1 cup flour
- ♥ pinch of salt
- ♥ 1 teaspoon baking powder
- ♥ sliced apples

Cream the butter and sugar, add the beaten egg and milk, mix in the flour, salt and baking powder, and pour into a pudding basin which has been filled with sliced apples. And don't put any sugar on those apples when you slice them. Just pour the batter over, cover and steam for 2 hours.

FATHER'S APPLE PUDDING

My father also made an apple pudding sometimes and, of course, he did put cloves in it. He was a good cook, my father. He had spent the greater part of his life on a cattle station up beyond Oodnadatta. It belonged to his uncle to whom he went as a Jackaroo when he was still in his teens, and from whom he eventually inherited the property. Going off and helping relatives seems to have been a tradition in my family – a sort of "extended family" pattern. That doesn't seem to happen these days. Anyway it was here that my father learned to cook, but I don't suppose there was much place for haute cuisine in station life in those days, so what he made was plain and simple. But he enjoyed cooking and so it was also always extremely good. There is nothing quite as comforting as this pudding on a cold and hungry night.

Fill a pudding bowl about ³/₄ full with sliced apples. Sugar them a little and add a few cloves, some lemon juice and a lump of butter. Rub 3 oz. of suet into 6 oz. of flour, to which has been added ¹/₂ teaspoon baking powder and a pinch of salt. Mix in enough water to make a stiff dough. Pat out to the size of your pudding basin, and sit it atop the apples. Steam for 1 hour. This was always served with a thin custard, never cream.

And now is the moment, I think, to explain to you, my children, how to make a boiled custard, a useful accomplishment which people seem to have forgotten these days. I think I feel about it a little the way my mother felt about her white sauce. There is a right way to make it and here it is.

Take from 1¹/₂ cups milk sufficient to mix smooth 1 teaspoon of cornflour. Heat gently the remainder of the milk with 2 tablespoons sugar. Beat 2 large eggs well and mix into them the cornflour and milk. When the milk is almost boiling, add to it the egg mixture and stir until the first bubbles appear. Remove from the fire and add vanilla, rum, brandy or whatever flavour you prefer. If you want a thicker custard, use an extra egg, a little more cornflour, or a little less milk. More sugar, too, if you want it sweeter.

URNEY PUDDING

Our gardener had a small son named Ernie, and I always thought this pudding had something to do with him, particularly as my mother usually made it with apricot jam so it came out a colour vaguely reminiscent of Ernie's hair. I was very surprised when I finally saw the recipe written and realised how it was spelled.

It is a recipe I have always liked not just because it tastes good, but because I was fascinated by all that weighing of eggs. ("What would happen Mother, if you had one very big egg and one very small one?" "Don't ask silly questions dear, and pass me the jam.") I wasn't quite so fascinated with it in New York where my kitchen was not equipped for weighing. American recipes are in cup measurements. At home, we had one of those scales where you put the weights on one side and the thing you were weighing in the tray on the other, the eggs were put where the weights usually went, and there was always the possibility that they'd roll off and break. That was another fascination. In case you don't want to go through the egg-weighing process I now work on the assumption that a normal-sized egg weighs approximately 2 oz. but it is more fun the other way.

- ♥ 2 eggs and their weight in butter and SR flour
- ♥ the weight of 1 egg in sugar
- ♥ 2 tablespoons jam

Cream the butter and sugar, add the beaten eggs and fold in the flour then the jam. Steam for 2 hours.

SAGO PLUM PUDDING

A pudding we often had in winter time was this one – moist and not too sweet, and always served with cream. It was a very usual pudding. Everybody's mother made it. But I do not now have a printed cookbook which gives the recipe, and so in case you don't either, I offer you my mother's way of doing it.

- ♥ 2 tablespoons sago, soaked overnight in 1 cup milk
- ♥ 1 cup soft breadcrumbs
- ♥ 1 cup sultanas
- ♥ $1/2$ cup sugar
- ♥ $1/2$ teaspoon carb. soda dissolved in a little milk
- ♥ 2 tablespoons melted butter

Mix all the ingredients together in the order given. Steam for $2^{1}/_{2}$ hours.

♥ ♥

BRIDIE'S PLUM PUDDING

My mother once got herself to Ireland simply by being in the right place at the right moment. As a young girl, she was having tea with an aunt who told her that that very morning she had received a letter from another aunt who lived in Ireland. The Irish aunt wrote to say she and her husband were getting old and wished they could have someone to live with them as a companion. She was suggesting that my mother's cousin, Gwynneth, might go. "I don't suppose she will", the Australian aunt said sadly, "she's much too busy with her university work". "What a pity", my mother replied, "I'd go if I were asked". And in the end, go she did, and remained happily there for some years. She brought back with her this recipe.

- ♥ 3 cups flour
- ♥ 1 cup sugar
- ♥ 1 cup raisins
- ♥ 1 cup currants
- ♥ 2 teaspoons carb. soda
- ♥ 2 tablespoons butter
- ♥ 2 cups boiling water
- ♥ nutmeg and lemon peel

Mix all well together and leave overnight. Boil for 3 hours.

♥ ♥

My Granny Vaughan's cookbook gives a recipe so similar that I feel it must have the same ancestry. Perhaps it was a family recipe which Granny had adapted slightly. Hers makes a smaller, lighter pudding. She used:

- 1 dessertspoon carb. soda
- 1 cup flour
- 1 cup breadcrumbs
- a little grated lemon peel
- 1 cup sugar
- 1 cup raisins
- 1 tablespoon butter
- good pinch salt and nutmeg

Her method of mixing was to pour ½ cup boiling water over the soda and then this over the butter. Then she said "toss this into the other ingredients". Leave overnight and boil 3 hours.

It was after my mother returned from Ireland that she and my aunt were on the Toorak Station in Melbourne when they espied an acquaintance a little way along the platform. "And who's that handsome man with her?" demanded my aunt who had an eye for the gentlemen. It turned out to be my father.

SUET PUDDING

My father had a very light hand with suet pudding. Perhaps he had had lots of practice up there on the station, where flour and beef suet were probably things always to hand. His method was simplicity itself.

- ♥ ½ cup of suet
- ♥ 1 cup SR flour
- ♥ a little sugar and a pinch of salt
- ♥ ¼ cup milk

Rub the finely chopped suet into the flour, sugar and salt, mix with the milk and steam for 1 hour. Hot golden syrup or jam was what went with this.

ANNIE'S SPOTTED DICK

My father didn't consider this a "proper" suet pudding – it was much too fancy – but it was always my favourite. I used to have it at the house of a friend, whose maid Annie made it and was eventually persuaded to part with the recipe. I'll bet I was the only 12-year-old who ever pestered her for one of her recipes. I hope she was flattered. I have it still in my recipe book, written in a surprisingly jaunty hand. I remember her as a very sombre person.

- ♥ 5 oz. flour
- ♥ 1/2 teaspoon baking powder
- ♥ pinch of salt
- ♥ 3 oz. suet
- ♥ 2 oz. sugar
- ♥ 3 oz. sultanas
- ♥ nutmeg
- ♥ 3/4 gill milk

Have a boiler of water on in readiness. Flour a pudding cloth. Sift the flour, baking powder and salt. Remove the skin from the suet, flake it and chop finely. Add the suet, sugar, sultanas and grated nutmeg to the flour. Mix well together. Mix to a stiff dough with the milk, using a wooden spoon. Tie up firmly in cloth, allowing room to swell. Boil for 1 1/2 hours. Serve with sweet sauce.

Remember, this recipe was given me when I was 12. The sky will not fall if you use packet suet and save yourself the trouble of skinning and flaking. And you don't have to use a cloth, though I like it better that way. Incidentally, the "sweet sauce" Annie refers to was made like a thin white sauce with a little sugar and brandy added.

MRS BOWDEN'S STEAM PUDDING

Mrs Bowden was one of mother's bridge-playing friends. She was, Mother said, a very good bridge player, but she was renowned in our house for two quite different things. The first was that she had – or at least said she had – once sent her son out with lace frills sewn round the bottom of his trousers, for some misdemeanour I can't now remember. It says much for her charm, I think, that we children liked her despite this. Perhaps it was due to her second claim to fame – Mrs Bowden's Steam Pudding. Although I always liked this, it wasn't until I grew up and had to juggle my own household budget that I realised why we had it so often. It's light, good, very filling ... and cheap. Need I say more.

- ♥ 1 tablespoon butter, margarine or dripping
- ♥ 1 tablespoon sugar
- ♥ 2 tablespoons jam
- ♥ 1 teaspoon carb. soda
- ♥ ½ cup milk
- ♥ 1 cup plain flour

Cream the butter and sugar, and add jam. Dissolve the carb. soda in the milk, and add to the mixture alternately with the flour. Steam for 2 hours.

ORANGE PUDDING

Aunt made a good and fairly economical steamed orange pudding which we liked too. In her recipe book she has written beside it "this can be baked or steamed", but she gives no instructions for baking, and as far as I know she always steamed it.

- ♥ 1 tablespoon butter
- ♥ 2 tablespoons sugar
- ♥ grated rind of 1 large orange
- ♥ 1 egg
- ♥ 1 cup milk
- ♥ 1 cup SR flour
- ♥ pinch of salt

Cream the butter and sugar, add the orange rind and egg, and beat to a cream, then add milk, alternately with the flour and some salt. Steam for 1 hour, and serve with the following sauce:

- ♥ 2 tablespoons butter
- ♥ 1/2 cup sugar
- ♥ juice of 1/2 lemon
- ♥ juice of 1 orange
- ♥ grated rind of 1/2 orange
- ♥ 1 dessertspoon cornflour
- ♥ 1 cup water
- ♥ 1/2 cup sherry

Cream the butter and sugar and add to it the juice of the lemon and orange and the orange rind. With 1 cup of water, dissolve the cornflour in a little of the water, then add the rest and cook, stirring, until boiling and thickened. Pour this over the butter and sugar mixture and beat for 5 minutes. When ready to serve, reheat, but don't boil. Add the sherry at the last minute.

GOLDEN DUMPLINGS

This is one of my mother's recipes, which I grew up with and so did you. She used to say it was wonderful because if you put it on just as you sat down to your first course, it was cooked precisely at the moment when you'd finished that and were ready for the next. When I made this same remark to Frances, who asked for the recipe when she was at university, both she and her flatmate fell about with mirth. Who ever heard of taking 20 minutes over your first course, they asked. Well, we did. Either we ate slower, or more.

In a fit of experimentation, I once tried making these dumplings with lemon and extra sugar instead of golden syrup, but it tasted like cough mixture. Sometimes old ways are best.

FOR THE SYRUP:
- 1 cup water
- 1 tablespoon golden syrup
- 1 tablespoon butter
- ½ cup sugar

Put into a saucepan and boil.

FOR THE DUMPLINGS:
- 1 tablespoon butter
- 1 cup SR flour
- 1 egg
- a little milk

Rub the butter into the flour, and add the egg and sufficient milk to make a soft dough. Roll into balls. Drop into the boiling syrup, cover and cook for 20 minutes.

COLD

Very few of our cold puddings were made with gelatine. I thought mother didn't like it much but it now occurs to me, going through her old cookbooks – the printed ones and the early parts of her own handwritten one – that perhaps gelatine was more difficult to cope with then. So many of the recipes include instructions which I'd find impossible to follow like "soak the isinglass in claret for ½ an hour", or "always use sheet gelatine". However, we did have jellies. My mother liked them made with fruit. How I wish I still had the small white earthenware mould she always used to set them in. My aunt always maintained she liked them best clear and plain. But "plain" is a misnomer for they were certainly never made, as they usually are today, with water, gelatine and artificial flavouring. When I was really very small, I had my tonsils out, and an aunt of my mother's offered to bring me some of her port wine jelly. My mother pointed out that I was only a little girl and maybe wine wasn't good for me. "Dearie", said her aunt firmly, "you can't make jelly without wine". Alas, now you can. It's a great pity. There was one which mother did make without wine, but its accompaniment more than compensated for it. This was coffee jelly, and although I have no recipe for it, I believe she did it like this.

To 1 pint of strong, hot black coffee, add sugar to taste. Dissolve 1 level tablespoon of gelatine in a little cold water, and stir it into the coffee until dissolved. Pour into a mould and leave to set. Turn out and serve with plenty of whipped cream, well flavoured with brandy.

PARADISE PUDDING

As I grew older, making the pudding was often my responsibility, and I was always ready to try something new. Mother was not as keen on this as I was, since they didn't always turn out as I expected, and then she had to do something herself at the last minute. A dinner without pudding was unthinkable, of course. However, Paradise Pudding was one of my more successful efforts, although I have no recollection of where I originally found the recipe. A newspaper perhaps? I could never resist trying what those women's pages spoke of in such glowing terms, though I have a feeling mother felt this was a very doubtful source of supply. As I've said before, she liked to have names attached to her recipes.

- ♥ 1 oz. soft breadcrumbs
- ♥ 3 oz. sugar
- ♥ 3 oz. currants
- ♥ 3 apples, peeled and grated
- ♥ a little nutmeg
- ♥ rind of 1/2 lemon
- ♥ pinch of salt
- ♥ 3 eggs

Mix all the ingredients together except the eggs. Beat these well, and then add, mixing in well. Put in a buttered and sugared basin, cover and steam for 1 1/2 hours.

ANGEL FOOD

A simple one this. Sometimes called Spanish Cream. Maybe that's its real name and we just attributed it to the angels because we liked it. I often made this for you children when you were small, but we always had it for birthdays and special events.

- ❤ 1 dessertspoon gelatine
- ❤ 2 eggs
- ❤ 2 tablespoons sugar
- ❤ 1 pint milk
- ❤ vanilla

Soak the gelatine in a little cold water. Separate the eggs and beat the yolks and sugar, then return to the saucepan with the milk and stir until it boils and separates. Take off at once, add the vanilla and fold in the stiffly beaten egg whites. Fold in the gelatine. Pour into a mould and when set, turn out onto a plate.

FLUMMERY

I don't know where Mother found the recipe for this one. It suddenly seems to have appeared when I was about 16, and not only on our table, but on most other people's, too. It was a nuisance to beat – we all took a hand at that – but it was good, easy and light. Excellent for summer.

Mix 1 heaped tablespoon of flour in 1 cup of cold water very smoothly. Strain the juice from a small tin of pineapple and, if necessary, add water to bring it up to 1 cup. Add this to the flour and water together with 1 cup of sugar and 1 heaped tablespoon of powdered gelatine. Bring to the boil, stirring all the time. Add the juice of 2 oranges and 1 lemon. Turn into a basin and allow to cool. When beginning to set, beat for $1/2$ hour until it is thick and fluffy. Add 6 passionfruit and the chopped pineapple. Turn into a bowl to set. Any fruit of course can be used, but if you can get passionfruit, this is really the best combination I think. It serves at least six.

❤ ❤

MRS HARVEY'S SISTER-IN-LAW

I have no idea who Mrs Harvey was, let alone her sister-in-law, but all my life this is what this particular recipe has been called. It used to amuse us greatly to have it when our friends came to dinner, so we could ask them, quite seriously, "Will you have a little of Mrs Harvey's Sister-in-Law?" Though, of course, to us it really was no joke. We had known it that way for so long that there didn't seem anything peculiar about it. Once, at one of the many schools Frances has been to in many parts of the world, she had to take a cooking class as part of the ordinary curriculum. She was not too cooperative about it, as she maintained she knew everything they were teaching her, and the whole thing came to a head one day when she arrived home utterly disgusted. "They said they were going to teach us how to make Lemon Sponge", she announced. "And you know what it turned out to be? Mrs Harvey's Sister-in-Law." As far as our family is concerned, that's its real name.

❤ ❤

❤❤❤❤❤❤❤❤❤❤❤❤❤❤❤❤❤❤❤❤❤❤❤❤❤❤❤❤❤❤

- ♥ 1 cup sugar
- ♥ 2 rounded tablespoons cornflour
- ♥ 2 eggs
- ♥ 1 lemon, grated rind and juice
- ♥ 1/2 pint milk
- ♥ vanilla

Put 2 cups water and sugar on to boil. Mix the cornflour with a little water, and add it to the sugar and water. Stir until it thickens and is smooth. Take off the fire and allow to cool, while beating the egg whites to a stiff froth. Stir them and the sugar mixture carefully into the lemon and pour into a bowl to set. Rinse the bowl out with cold water first, so you can easily turn it out. When it is cold, turn it onto a plate and pour over it a custard which you have made with the egg yolks, half a pint of milk, sugar and vanilla to taste.

❤❤❤❤❤❤❤❤❤❤❤❤❤❤❤❤❤❤❤❤❤❤❤❤❤❤❤❤❤❤❤

Custards in various shapes and forms played a big part in our cold pudding repertoire. This one was my aunt's own invention, and was named after the house where she lived and must so often have produced it. It is surprisingly simple. It tastes delicious.

ARDMORE PUDDING

Make a very good baked custard, by beating 3 eggs into a pint of rich milk, adding sugar to taste and a little vanilla. Stand the dish in another of water, and bake until it is set and browned on top. Allow it to get quite cold, then spread carefully over it a thin layer of apricot jam, and over the top of that a thick layer of whipped cream.

CARAMEL CUSTARD

This was another of Aunt's specialities. At least the recipe was always referred to as Ruby's Caramel Custard although mostly my mother made it. My own fondness for it can be judged by the fact that once when Mother went off on one of her very rare holidays without us, leaving me and my father to cope with the meals, my very last plaintive cry to her was not "Have a good time" or "Come back soon", but "I forgot to ask how to make Caramel Custard". As the train drew out of the station my mother, leaning far out the window waving to us, could be heard calling, "Set the dish in the top of a saucepan of water and it takes about half an hour".

Put 3/4 cup caster sugar in the bottom of a round cake tin which will hold rather more than a pint. Put this on top of the stove until the sugar is melted and of a bright brown colour, then pour on a custard made of a pint of milk, 2 or 3 eggs, well beaten,

1½ tablespoons sugar and a little vanilla essence. Have a saucepan of boiling water, in which to stand the tin, cover and let it steam till it is set. From ½ to ¾ hour ought to do it. Let it stand until quite cold and turn out.

A double boiler will make this all right but it is far easier to turn out if you use a round cake tin of the size my aunt indicates and which will fit neatly into the top of a saucepan, with the saucepan lid on top of it. Of course, some people bake it in the oven, and in that case, you stand your container in another of water and don't cover it. To me, steaming is still the right way, though.

POLKA PUDDING

Mother made another cold custard pudding I liked, Polka Pudding. It doesn't really seem to be much more than glorified blanc mange, but then there's nothing wrong with a good blanc mange is there? We used to have that often, served with cherry jam and whipped cream. There's more of a richness to Polka Pudding though. Mother always set it in a narrow earthenware mould, so that it came to the table tall and fluted and turreted like a small castle.

- ♥ 3 tablespoons cornflour
- ♥ 1½ pints milk
- ♥ lemon rind
- ♥ 2 eggs
- ♥ 1 oz. butter
- ♥ ½ cup sugar
- ♥ flavouring

Mix the cornflour smoothly with a little of the milk, and put the rest on to boil, with a thin slice of lemon rind in it. Beat the eggs well and add to the cornflour. When the milk is hot, but not quite boiling, stir in the butter, sugar and then the egg mixture. Stir until it is thick and then pour into a wet mould. When cold and set, turn out. I have also found this recipe in the old *Goulburn Cook Book*, but here for flavouring they suggest "Peach leaves give it a nice flavour". I must say I've never tried that, but we had a bay tree growing in our garden and mother often boiled a fresh green bay leaf in the milk for a custard, and that was very good.

FLOATING ISLAND

Even in the days when the only food Kate really liked was fried chicken and apple pie, she appreciated Floating Island, and although her horizons have broadened somewhat since then it is still a favourite. It was a great bond, therefore, when her sister married someone who felt the same way about it. The recipe I make came from that source of inspiration and good food, the Rudolph Steiner School in New York.

- ❤ 3 eggs
- ❤ 7 tablespoons sugar
- ❤ 1/8 teaspoon salt
- ❤ 2 cups milk, scalded
- ❤ 1/2 teaspoon vanilla
- ❤ nutmeg

Separate the eggs. Add 1 tablespoon sugar to the whites and beat until stiff. Beat the yolks with 6 tablespoons sugar and salt. Slowly stir in the hot milk and add the vanilla. Pour this into a double boiler and cook, stirring constantly until the custard coats the spoon. (That's the sort of instruction my mother issued, only she always said until it coats a silver spoon.) If custard starts to curdle remove from heat and beat with an egg beater. (Mother never told me that one. If it curdled, there was nothing for it but to hang your head and slink off.) Pour custard into serving dish. Put the beaten egg whites into the same pan and heat over double boiler for a few minutes to make firm. Make "islands" with spoonfuls of the whites upon the custard lake. Sprinkle with nutmeg. Serve cold.

RUBY'S LEMON SAGO

My aunt seems to have been the pudding queen, for this is her recipe too. It is fashionable not to like sago these days, but we had it often in a variety of ways. This was the way I liked it best.

- ♥ 1 cup sago
- ♥ 1 cup sugar
- ♥ 2 tablespoons golden syrup
- ♥ grated rind and juice of 2 lemons

Soak the sago in 4 cups of water for about an hour. Add to it the sugar, golden syrup and lemon rind. Simmer until the sago is clear and add the lemon juice. Mix well and pour into serving bowl. Serve cold with whipped cream.

TASMANIAN SEMOLINA PUDDING

This came from my mother's childhood in Tasmania, so it is an old one. Good though. Better in fact than the recipe might lead you to believe. And inexpensive. I was surprised in copying this from my mother's book to see that bit about raspberry jam and cream. I think we always had it plain.

> Put 2 oz. semolina and 4 to 5 oz. sugar in a saucepan. Pour in a cup of cold water and, after stirring, add a cup of hot water. Boil quickly for 5 minutes, stirring all the time. Take off the fire and add grated rind and juice of half a lemon. Pour into a basin and when cool (but not cold) beat for 10 minutes. Put into a glass dish and garnish with raspberry jam and whipped cream.

People had time for that 10-minute beating in those days, or else there were plenty of children about to lend a hand. It may take less time now with electric beaters, but you will know when it is ready for it whips up surprisingly white and creamy.

EGG PUDDING

You see, even the cold ones were referred to as puddings. I always find "pudding" such a glum word, and yet it covered everything, even something as light and airy as this one. It used to seem to me that mashed bananas, sugar and cream was such a good combination I wondered why people didn't serve it at elegant dinner parties, instead of reserving it for nursery teas. Banana sandwiches are good too. And at one time, we used to make delicious little crustless cheese sandwiches, soak them in egg and milk, fry them crisp and eat them with mashed banana and cinnamon. I think you have to be in your teens to appreciate that one. But I have wandered far from the point, which is Egg Pudding, a quite close relative of mashed banana and cream, and suitable for the most elegant table.

Beat the whites of 4 eggs until stiff. Beat the 4 yolks with 1/2 cup sugar and add the grated rind and juice of 1 large lemon, 1 large mashed banana and 1 dessertspoon of gelatine melted in a little water. Beat all very well together, preferably with an electric mixer or blender. Then fold in the egg whites, pour into a serving bowl and refrigerate. To serve, top with whipped cream, flavoured with a little rum or brandy, and sprinkle with slivered, toasted almonds. You can make this the day before, but personally I prefer to do it the same day I am serving it. Bananas don't like to wait.

CRÊT BÉRARD CARAMEL APPLES

Crêt Bérard is a retreat House in Switzerland in beautiful mountain country above the vineyards that climb up behind Lausanne, with a heavenly view across the lake to the Dents du Midi, beyond. I was there for meetings some years ago, and now my collection is the richer by at least three recipes, carefully written out in French and marked "Recette donnée par la cuisinière de Crêt-Bérard". Here is the best one.

- ♥ 6 apples
- ♥ 3½ oz. sugar
- ♥ 1 teaspoon cornflour
- ♥ ³/₈ cup cream
- ♥ 2 oz. almonds, peeled slivered and browned

Peel the apples, cut them in half and take out the cores. Caramelise the sugar and gently pour on to it 2 cups of cold water, stirring. Cook the apples in this sauce just until they are tender. Take them out gently so as not to break them and arrange them in a serving dish. Dissolve the cornflour in a little water and add it to the sauce, stirring while it thickens. Let it cook for 3 minutes and then take off the fire and allow to cool slightly. Then add the cream and pour over the apples. Decorate with the almonds. Serve cold.

GOOSEBERRY FOOL

It always seems to me that the first gooseberries of the season are meant for Gooseberry Fool. You children moaned every time I mentioned it, and your father said the only thing gooseberries were meant for was pie, but I have never quite recovered from the habit. We did have gooseberry pie, and Mother always made gooseberry jam (Cape Gooseberry jam was the best in the world!) but the first gooseberries were always for Fool. When I see other recipes for fruit fool, I realise that Mother had her own way of doing it – perhaps from economy – but it was very good all the same, and is still the way I make it today. To the best of my knowledge mother had no written recipe for what she did, and so I simply follow what I remember her doing, and the result is fairly vague as to quantities. I usually use a punnet of gooseberries, or if they are very small punnets, two.

Make a custard with 3/4 cup of milk and one egg, a little sugar and vanilla to flavour.

Do not bother to top and tail the gooseberries, but simply wash them and boil them in a very little water. When they are cooked, put them through a sieve and throw out the skins. Into the hot gooseberry purée stir enough sugar to sweeten, and about 1/2 cup of fine white breadcrumbs to give a little body. Then leave to get quite cold. Mix in the custard. Whip 1/2 cup of heavy cream, and fold it into the gooseberries. Cover the top with grated nutmeg.

SUMMER PUDDING

This is another memory of childhood, for which I have no actual recipe. Mother always made it with those soft rather squashy mulberries which grow in South Australia but which aren't the same as mulberries in many other parts of the world. I make it with blackberries, which I don't think are as good. But then whatever is as good as our childhood memories? I think you can make it with any of the summer berries, and maybe even cherries or plums. What you do is simplicity itself, and why it should taste as good as it does I don't know. Another of those miracles in which good kitchens abound.

Line a basin with slices of bread, cutting small pieces to fill up the crevices so it is all covered. Stew the fruit with sugar and not too much water.

Pour while still very hot into the centre of the bread, filling right to the top if possible and keeping out a little of the hot juice. Cover the top with more slices of bread and pour the remainder of the juice over the top so all the bread is saturated. Put a plate on top so it is pressed down a little. When cold, put in the refrigerator and leave overnight. Turn out carefully and serve with whipped cream.

MARJORIE'S MOCHA CREAM

This was one of the first recipes Marjorie ever gave me, and I don't feel I can leave it out. Your father, while spooning up the absolute last mouthful, used to say it looked like a Sunday School picnic. It didn't taste like one, and as a matter of fact it didn't look like any I ever went to, but maybe I was deprived.

Butter a basin well, and line with sponge cake cut about 3/8 inch thick. Cream 1/4 lb. butter with 1/2 lb. sugar until very light. Beat in 3 small eggs, then – drop by drop – 1 tablespoon coffee essence. Be careful, if you're impatient, you'll curdle it. Put a layer of this cream on sponge cake, then cake again, and so on until the cream is used, allowing more depth of cream than cake. Let the top layer be cake. Place a plate on top and leave for 24 hours in the fridge. Unmould, and mask with whipped cream. Decorate with cherries and almonds. For larger quantities, it is safer to weigh the eggs and use the same weight in butter and sugar.

SOPHIE'S APRICOT CREAM

Once a year, in November, Sophie and I had what we called our Creature Party. The creature was venison of some sort, usually chevreuil, and it was my job to prepare it. Sophie's was to top and tail those very thin, green beans which is an endless job if you are cooking for eight, and also to make the afters. This is what she usually did. It really is a truer Fool than Mother's gooseberry one, but that's not what she called it.

Soak 4 oz. of dried apricots in water overnight. Drain, and cook them in a little water until very soft, then blend them or put them through a sieve or a mouli grinder. Add sugar to taste and stir to dissolve it. Allow to get quite cold. Whip a cup of heavy cream and stir into the cold apricots. Whip 1 egg white stiff with a dessertspoon sugar, and fold that into the apricots too. Pile in your serving dish. Sophie doesn't say so, but a few toasted, slivered almonds go well, sprinkled over the top. A bit of crunch is a good thing.

Sometimes we had cold jam tart and cream for pudding. But there were two other kinds of tart fillings which Mother sometimes made and which I infinitely preferred. One of them was made with

MOTHER'S LEMON BUTTER

There were always several jars of this stored on the cellar shelves along with the jam, green tomato or cauliflower pickles, salted beans, and the big brown stone jars of pickled onions. We children used to like to eat it on bread and butter if we got the chance. But that wasn't often. Mother considered it too expensive to be used indiscriminately. It is expensive too – not because of what goes into it so much as how little it makes. Always less than I anticipate. On the other hand it is the best I know. Sometimes it was put between layers of fresh sponge cake and served for tea, but the way I liked it best was in small individual tart cases, the filling baked right along with the pastry, and topped, when cold, with a dab of whipped cream.

- ♥ 6 oz. butter
- ♥ 1 lb. sugar
- ♥ 6 eggs
- ♥ 5 lemons

Melt the butter and sugar in a saucepan standing in another containing boiling water. (I guess my mother, when she wrote this, didn't own a double boiler which is, of course, what I use for it.) Then add eggs, well beaten and strained, the lemon juice (also strained), and the peel, very finely grated. Stir till it thickens and then pour into jars. Cover when cold.

RUBY'S ORANGE FILLING

The other tart filling I adored came from my Aunt Ruby. I have never seen it in any recipe book, or even anything like it. Perhaps she made it up. It is very good, and quite apart from serving it at my own table I have found it an easy and excellent thing to make for church fêtes and PTA cake stalls.

Line a pie plate with short crust. Cover the bottom with a round of grease-proof paper weighed down with rice and bake lightly.

Fill with the following mixture (after you've removed the rice and paper of course).

Cream together 1 dessertspoon butter and 1 cup sugar. Add 1 egg, the grated rind and juice of 1 orange, and 2 apples, peeled, cored and grated. Bake in a moderate oven until set and a little brown on top.

BUSHWHACKER'S TART

This was another tart we sometimes had, though it was not always served cold. Warm, with a little whipped cream is good. Despite its outback title, it was not one of my father's recipes – which were all much simpler – but came from another friend from the Oodnadatta days, known to absolutely everybody as Aunt Ethel. I always enjoyed her because she was full of fun and full of stories, about all sorts of people I never met but in the end felt I knew. She could also read tea cups, and did frequently. She once told me, at a time when I was planning on marrying a farmer and settling down on the land, that she could see me riding a camel and having a high old time in the desert. I haven't done either of those things yet, but I suppose there's always time.

Make ½ lb. of good pastry and with it line small pattypans or one large tart plate.

MIX TOGETHER:
- ♥ 4 tablespoons currants
- ♥ 4 tablespoons sugar
- ♥ small piece candied peel, chopped finely
- ♥ 2 tablespoons apricot jam

Put a little of this into each little pattypan, or all into the big tart plate.

BEAT TOGETHER:
- ♥ 2 oz. butter
- ♥ 4 oz. sugar
- ♥ 1 egg
- ♥ and add 4 oz. coconut

Pour this over the fruit mixture, and bake in a moderate oven for about 20 minutes.

CHESS PIE WITH MARRONS

Of much later vintage is this, which is another of those good things which came so regularly from Bill and Ruth's New York kitchen.

- ♥ 2 oz. sugar
- ♥ 2 eggs
- ♥ 6 oz. butter
- ♥ 8 or 10 preserved marrons

- ♥ 2 tablespoons light cream
- ♥ 2 tablespoons flour
- ♥ 1 teaspoon vanilla

Combine all the ingredients except the marrons, beat well and pour into an unbaked pie shell. Cut the marrons in halves or quarters and distribute evenly over the pie. Bake at 325°F for about 40 minutes or until golden brown.

BUTTER TARTS

There used to be a time when I loved Butter Tarts so much I issued an edict, "No one must come down to New York from Toronto without bringing me butter tarts". And mostly nobody did. Frances certainly never dared to come back from university without them. They were delicious, and Toronto is the only place I've ever found them, although they may be available all over Canada. To me, they are strictly a Canadian institution, though perhaps related to the American Pecan Pie. Now that I am too far away for people to bring them to me, some kind friend has provided the recipe.

Line small pattypans with good rich pie crust, and fill with the following mixture:

- 3 tablespoons soft butter
- ⅓ cup lightly packed brown sugar
- ⅓ cup corn syrup
- 1 egg
- pinch salt
- ½ teaspoon vanilla
- 1 teaspoon vinegar
- ½ cup raisins

Cream the butter, blend in the sugar and add the corn syrup. Beat the egg and add with salt. Add the vanilla, vinegar and raisins. Bake at 400°F until lightly brown. If you like a runnier mixture use a little more corn syrup.

PANCAKES AND FRITTERS

As well as baked, boiled and cold, there were also pancakes and fritters, though we had these less often. The trouble was, of course, that they involved my mother going out to the kitchen between one course and another and cooking them. First of all there were:

APPLE FRITTERS

- ♥ 2 oz. flour
- ♥ 1 egg, separated
- ♥ pinch of salt
- ♥ 1 dessertspoon melted butter
- ♥ apples

Put the flour in a basin and make a well in the middle. Drop in the egg yolk and mix carefully, then add the melted butter and 1/2 wine glass tepid water. That 1/2 wine glass is a little tricky, of course, but you'll be all right if you add the water a little at a time until it is the right consistency. Let it stand for an hour. Just before using, beat the egg white with the pinch of salt until stiff and fold in. Peel and core the apples, keeping them whole. Slice them across into rings about 1/2 inch thick, dip into the batter and fry in plenty of fat until the batter is golden and the apples cooked through. The sugar bowl was passed with these, so that each person sprinkled sugar according to their taste.

Sometimes these fritters were made with bananas instead of apples. In this case you sliced the banana into the batter and cooked it in spoonfuls.

But best of all were

PANCAKES

Since those far off days of my childhood I have had to do with many pancakes of many varieties. The stacked buckwheat kind you eat for breakfast in the States with maple syrup, bacon and those small crisp sausages. The ones you stuff with something savoury and serve with a sauce. The thin crepes you cook at the table and flambé with a delicious perfume of orange and brandy. All are good, but for me "pancakes" are what my mother made. It was quite a performance the night we ate them, and that was part of the fun, too. The batter was made ahead of time, and left to "rest", covered with one of those circles of white mosquito net surrounded by crocheted lattice work and weighed down with blue beads.

- ♥ salt
- ♥ 2 oz. flour
- ♥ 2 eggs
- ♥ 1 small cup milk
- ♥ butter

Sift the salt and flour into a small basin, and make a well in the middle. Into this, drop the eggs and a little of the milk and mix to a smooth paste. Then add enough of the remaining milk to make a mixture about the consistency of thick cream. After it has had its hour's rest, it will need thinning a little more, and you can add the rest of the milk. It should be thin cream by the time you're ready to cook it in the melted butter.

By the time my mother was ready to cook it, the "assembly line" was ready on the kitchen table too. A plateful of butter cut into small cubes. A little bowl of caster sugar with a spoon in it. Lemon, cut ready for squeezing. And my brother, all set to do his part. For some reason it was always he who helped with pancake making. Perhaps because he liked it, or perhaps (perish the thought) he was better at it than I. When the great moment arrived to eat, then began the cooking and assembling. Mother had – as indeed now have I – one particular small frying pan which she always used for pancakes. It was the right size. The right weight. It was the "pancake pan".

When she had it hot on the fire, then she dropped in a small piece of butter, letting it melt but not brown, and ran it round the pan, just coating the bottom. Into this, sizzling hot, went a tablespoon of batter, which also, with a supple wrist and still held over the fire, was run evenly all round the pan, covering the bottom with a thin layer. As it cooked and browned a little, a thin, flexible knife (one of those old, non-stainless-type knives all our mothers used, and oh how I wish I had one now!) was run under it and the pancake was flipped over with a quick movement of the wrist and a toss of the pan onto its other side. That took but a second to cook (the whole process is very quick) and the pancake was slid gently onto a heated plate, held waiting by my brother. This was the moment he went into action. While mother began on the second, my brother put a small cube of butter, a spoon of caster sugar and a squeeze of lemon in the centre of the first pancake, folded it over in three and rushed it to the table. We ate them one at a time, hot, as they came from the pan. By the time you finished your first one, the second was ready for you. My mother did not eat until all the rest of us had had ours. Her "seconds" were made by my brother, who was almost as good (and considerably more daring at the tossing of them) as my mother.

It is a nuisance perhaps having to cook them at the last minute like this, but they are more tender, hotter and more succulent than if you made them ahead of time and kept them hot. As far as I am concerned it is well worth the effort.

♥ ♥

MR VIRGIN'S FRITTERS

When my mother married that handsome man from the Toorak Station, she went with him to live on the station beyond Oodnadatta. I have always thought how very brave of her it was – a city girl born and bred – to go so far away from all she knew, into such primitive conditions, with her nearest neighbour fifty miles away or more. I suppose it was the same enterprising spirit that had sent her off so gaily to live with completely unknown relatives on the other side of the world. Strange how one never really knows one's parents. I always think of my very gentle mother as a timid woman. Certainly if you'd seen the way she locked up a house, you might have agreed with me. Absolutely every door (not to mention window) had its own key and was so firmly locked each night that opening up in the morning rather resembled freeing the Bastille.

At the time she married my father, the railway line from Adelaide only ran as far as Oodnadatta, so that from there on they had to go by horse and buggy, camping out each night or staying at one of the various stations along the way. Her recipe book bears witness to these journeys, with such things as Blood's Creek Gingernuts and this one from Mr Virgin, who was the cook at one of the stopovers.

♥ ♥

♥ ♥

- ♥ 2 oz. butter
- ♥ 2 oz. sugar
- ♥ 2 oz. flour
- ♥ half a pint milk
- ♥ 2 eggs
- ♥ ½ teaspoon baking powder
- ♥ pinch salt

Cream the butter and sugar and add the flour, milk and eggs. The flour and sugar should be warmed (!) and the baking powder and salt sifted with the flour. Mix well, and pour into small buttered enamel plates.

Bake for 25 minutes in a quick oven and serve with jam and cream.

Not always having a ready supply of small enamel plates, I use round flat cake tins for cooking these, folding the fritters over their jam cream filling like omelettes.

♥ ♥

CAKES

It was not until I got to America that I realised cakes could also be considered as "afters". We only had them for afternoon tea or supper. They were delicious, of course, but they weren't pudding. True, there were some puddings which were remarkably like cakes, but I never did like them much. I felt I was being had.

However, for the purpose of this book, I am putting cake recipes right here, because they are so often used as dessert these days, and because less and less in our busy lives, do we prepare the sort of enormous spreads we used to eat for afternoon tea. And the recipes are too good to lose.

Some of them, of course, are particularly suited for dessert. This one for instance.

HAZELNUT CAKE

This is the best nut cake I know, and I am particularly fond of nut cakes. It came from that same titled Viennese Lady, whose cooking demonstration gave my mother the Contessa's Beef Burgundy.

- ♥ 4 eggs
- ♥ 1/4 lb. caster sugar
- ♥ 1/2 lb. ground hazelnuts
- ♥ 2 or 3 tablespoons grated and sieved breadcrumbs
- ♥ 1/2 cup apricot jam
- ♥ 1 cup whipped cream

Put the eggs in a bowl and beat slightly. Add the sugar gradually and beat for 15 minutes with the egg beater. Then add the ground hazelnuts. Mix in well. Add the breadcrumbs. Place in a square cake tin about 2 inch deep and bake for 30 to 40 minutes in a moderate oven.

When cold, split the cake and spread with warmed apricot jam. Cover top of cake with the whipped cream.

I have been known to cook this in a round tin, with no dire consequences.

PAVLOVA CAKE

This also is more dessert than cake. If you are living overseas it is the great standby to produce when you want something truly Australian – unless you happen to be dealing with New Zealanders, who claim it as their national dish quite as vehemently as all Australians do.

My aunt has it written in her book as Marshmallow Cake, which describes it fairly accurately, but there's no doubt in my mind at all that its real name is Pavlova. Here is the way I make it.

- ♥ 3 egg whites
- ♥ 1 small cup sugar
- ♥ 1 teaspoon cornflour
- ♥ 1 teaspoon white vinegar

First prepare your tin. And perhaps my way of doing this is extraordinary, but it is the way my mother did it, and I find it best. Turn your cake tin upside down – I always use my Christmas cake tin which is a 10 inch one with a slight ridge round the edge when inverted – and cut 2 circles of brown paper to fit.

Just before putting the meringue mixture on it, I hold this brown paper under the cold water tap and smooth it wetly on top of the upside-down tin. Don't be tempted to cook it on a cookie sheet. It doesn't work.

Now, beat the egg whites stiff, and gradually add the sugar, beating in very well after every addition. Then carefully fold in the cornflour and the vinegar. Pour onto the wet brown paper and flatten evenly with a rubber spatula. Cook on the bottom shelf of a very cool oven for 1 hour. It should be crisp outside, but not browned. Allow to stand a moment to collect its thoughts, then invert it carefully onto a cake rack and remove the paper. When cold, slide it ever so gently onto its serving plate, fill its slightly sunken middle with whipped cream and cover with fruit. No fruit anywhere is as good with it as passionfruit, but strawberries, raspberries, tinned pineapple or bananas are delicious too.

GRANNY VAUGHAN'S POUND CAKE

Granny Vaughan, my mother's mother, was widowed when she was still in her twenties and left with two small girls, a house and not much money. Her husband had been a promising young lawyer, so what she did was to take in various highly respected members of the legal fraternity as "paying guests". When she died, she left a very healthy amount of money, very soundly invested. My mother said of her – rather primly – "Granny was always well advised". From all accounts my Granny Vaughan was a very beautiful young woman, and I expect there were many who were willing and eager to advise her.

This is one of her recipes. I like to think of her baking it for her legal men, and I am not surprised they were her friends for life after eating it. It is a good cake and keeps well – if you are strong minded enough not to eat it up the first week. Half the quantity makes one very large cake and for this I use 5 small eggs or 4 large ones and a little milk:

- 1¼ lb. butter
- 1 lb. caster sugar
- 9 eggs
- 1¼ lb. flour
- 1½ lb. raisins
- ¼ lb. lemon peel
- vanilla essence

Cream the butter and sugar, and add the beaten eggs, then flour, fruit and essence. Line the bottom of a deep tin with grease-proof paper and butter sides of tin. Pour in batter and cook in a slow oven for about 2 hours.

♥ ♥

MRS GATWOOD'S PLAIN CAKE

I don't know who Mrs Gatwood was, but she was certainly a most versatile lady. Hers was the recipe both my mother and my aunt used for almost every cake they ever made. Small cakes, layer cakes, log cakes – chocolate, orange or sultana – basically they all began with Mrs Gatwood. (When, many many years later, I bought my house from a Mrs Gatwood, I felt as if she were a life-long friend. She was apparently no relation, or at least I had considerable difficulty in explaining that I had always known her as a cake!)

When my mother had a bridge party, she would make Mrs Gatwood, dividing the mixture into 2 parts, making a layer cake out of one lot and little chocolate cream cakes out of the rest. Actually, my mother was renowned for those chocolate cream cakes. She baked them in small round flattish tins (probably tartlet tins, if everyone had their rights), iced the top with chocolate icing, then scooped out a spoonful

♥ ♥

♥ ♥

of cake, filled the hole with unsweetened whipped cream and sat the scooped-out hat of cake back on top. The batter was rich with chocolate, and because of the flattish shape there was always as much cream as cake. Luscious! But as I say, basically Mrs Gatwood's Plain Cake. So here she is.

- ♥ 1/4 lb. butter beaten to a cream with 1/2 lb. sugar
- ♥ 2 unbeaten eggs
- ♥ 1/2 small cup of milk and
- ♥ 1/2 lb. SR flour.

Mix all well together for a few minutes, and flavour to taste. Bake in a moderate oven for about 1/2 hour.

♥ ♥

EMMA'S SANDWICH

When our cakes were not Mrs Gatwood, they were Emma. I don't know who Emma was, any more than I know Mrs Gatwood, but her sandwich cake was part of my childhood. My mother considered Emma's Sandwich the best butter sponge cake of all time, and she was probably right.

- ♥ 4 oz. butter
- ♥ 5 oz. sugar
- ♥ 3 eggs
- ♥ 5 oz. SR flour

Beat the butter to a cream with the sugar. Add the eggs one at a time, beating well after each addition. Then sift in the flour gradually and beat well again. Cook in two small sandwich tins in a moderate oven for about 10 minutes. When cool put together with whatever filling you prefer, and ice. "Whatever filling you prefer" took in such things as jam, cream (or both together for special occasions), mother's lemon cheese or mock cream.

MOCK CREAM

From the books I have, it would seem that Australians are great ones for making mock. For making something out of something else. I have recipes for mock chicken, mock fish, mock ginger and – as I say – mock cream. Perhaps it was the pioneers trying to make the old familiar dishes from strange ingredients in a strange land. Perhaps it was the lean years of the Depression which taught that it was cheaper to make fish out of potatoes than to buy it in a fish shop. Some of these things are very good, though they don't often taste much like what they are meant to be. Mock cream is not as good as the real thing, but it is an excellent filling and a good standby, for there comes a time in all our lives when we have to substitute. So keep the recipe handy.

From $3/4$ cup milk keep out sufficient to mix smooth 1 dessertspoon of maizena. Boil the remaining milk and add maizena to it, stirring while it bubbles gently for a moment or two. Take off the fire and leave to cool, stirring from time to time to prevent a skin from forming.

Beat 1 tablespoon of butter with $1/4$ cup sugar to a cream. Add the milk and maizena mixture to this, a teaspoon at a time, beating in well after each addition, until all is mixed. Flavour with vanilla.

MRS WESTON'S CHOCOLATE CAKE

This is the famous Mrs Weston for whom I phoned from Sydney. She makes a very light, soft cake, and benefits from whipped cream between her layers and a good chocolate icing on top. It is a long time since I have had sour milk in my kitchen – milk now being made from heavens knows what instead of cows, and keeping forever – but Mrs Weston is very accommodating. She makes up just as well with fresh.

- ♥ $1/4$ lb. butter
- ♥ $1^{1/2}$ cups sugar
- ♥ 2 eggs, separated
- ♥ $1/2$ cup milk, sour if possible
- ♥ 2 cups SR flour
- ♥ $1/2$ teaspoon carb. soda
- ♥ $1/4$ cup cocoa

Cream the butter and sugar and add egg yolks, then milk and $1/2$ cup of hot water. Sift flour with carb. soda and cocoa, and add. Lastly fold in the beaten egg whites. This mixture makes 1 medium and 1 small sandwich cake. Bake in a moderate oven until cake tests done.

WALNUT AND GINGER CAKE

And here's one of about the same vintage which says firmly – "best baked in a square tin". It is, too.

- ♥ 4 oz. butter
- ♥ 4 oz. sugar
- ♥ 2 eggs
- ♥ 6 oz. SR flour
- ♥ 2 oz. each of walnuts and preserved ginger
- ♥ 1 dessertspoon of cocoa if liked

I don't ever remember it having cocoa, so perhaps my mother "didn't like". And I find that, despite the specific instruction about the shape of the tin, putting the cake together is left to your imagination. Mix in the usual way, it says. Oh well, I suggest creaming the butter and sugar, adding beaten eggs and then flour, nuts and ginger. And if you like, that dessertspoon of cocoa sifted with the flour. Put into its square tin and bake in a moderate oven until it tests done.

PEARL'S BROWN WALNUT CAKE

After their father died, both my mother and my aunt were sent to their maternal grandmother in Tasmania, and from then on spent a great deal of their time there. Holidays, I imagine, even when they were not actually living there. Those years are recorded in the recipe books by many entries which have in brackets after them the name, then (Tasmania). Pearl's Brown Walnut Cake is one of them. You have to be careful to cook it long enough. It is a big cake and if your tin is not perhaps as big as Pearl's was, and your batter therefore deeper, it will take longer. So treat her "hour or more" seriously.

- ♥ 1/2 lb. butter
- ♥ 1/2 lb. dark sugar
- ♥ 2 tablespoons golden syrup
- ♥ 2 eggs
- ♥ 1 teaspoon carb. soda dissolved in 1 tablespoon milk
- ♥ 11/2 cups chopped walnuts
- ♥ 21/2 cups flour

Cream the butter and sugar and golden syrup, then mix in the eggs. Add carb. soda and milk, and the chopped walnuts. Beat well together, then add the flour. Pour into a greased tin and bake in a moderate oven for an hour or more. Lard or butter can be used, or good dripping.

LYLE'S RUM AND WALNUT CAKE

Recipes come from all sources. This one was given me by the estate agent who sold us the first house we owned in Sydney – the one where Kate was born. She didn't just say out of the blue, "Now here's a house with a nice big kitchen, maybe you'd like a recipe or two to go with it". She and her family became our very good friends over the years we lived there, and some years had passed before she got round to giving me this recipe. It was one of her specialties and it's well worth the slight trouble of making it. I pass it on to you exactly as she wrote it down for me.

- ♥ 1 cup dates – cut in pieces
- ♥ ¼ cup good rum
- ♥ 1 teaspoon carb. soda
- ♥ ¼ lb. butter
- ♥ 1 cup sugar
- ♥ 2 eggs
- ♥ vanilla
- ♥ 1 cup walnuts
- ♥ 2 cups SR flour

Soak the dates overnight in rum and ¾ cup of water. If desired the proportion can be ¾ cup water and ¼ cup rum, or even half and half, but the proportion suggested is very good. You need 1 cup in all. In the morning, add carb. soda to the date mixture and beat. Allow to stand.

Cream the butter and sugar and add well beaten eggs. I add a small quantity of vanilla at this stage. Add the walnuts, broken into small pieces, to the date mixture and beat for a minute or two. Then add this to the butter and sugar. Lastly fold in the flour. Bake in a deep tin – I use a ring tin – for 1 hour in a moderate oven – a little more or less according to the heat of the oven.

The cake can be iced with coffee or rum-flavoured icing, or with

- ♥ 2 tablespoons milk
- ♥ 2 tablespoons butter
- ♥ 1 cup brown sugar

Boil all three together slowly for 5 minutes, without stirring. Put a few drops of rum into a basin, pour in the hot mixture and cool, for a few minutes only, then beat. The length of time you beat depends on your discretion, but I get best results from beating while it is still hot and not letting it become too thick. As it sets very quickly, I keep a cup of boiling water handy to dip my knife in to help with the spreading. This cake improves after a day or two but is delicious any time.

MILDURA TEA CAKE

My aunt once spent a holiday in Mildura, where much of Australia's dried fruit comes from. She brought back this recipe, which is one of the best things I know to serve with tea (or coffee) if you don't happen to care about calorie counting.

- ♥ 2 tablespoons each butter, sugar and milk
- ♥ 1 egg
- ♥ 5 tablespoons SR flour
- ♥ cinnamon, currants and raisins

Cream the butter and sugar, add egg and beat well. Add flour and milk. Put into a small sandwich tin, well buttered. Sprinkle the top with sugar, cinnamon, currants and raisins mixed together, and pop into a moderate oven, until it tests done – 10–15 minutes, it's not a thick cake. Immediately it comes out, split it in half, spread with butter and serve hot.

♥ ♥

Mother made a similar cake, but she cooked it plain, without topping. The moment it came out from the oven, she spread generous butter on its hot top, and quickly poured mixed cinnamon and sugar on as it melted. This also was served hot, but was good cold, too.

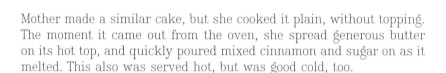

DAISY CAKE

There was always a cake in the oven on Sunday mornings, though how it managed to get there is now beyond me. When I remember the roasts and the vegetables and the puddings that went into that oven every Sunday, I wonder there was ever any room for a cake. I suppose it went in as the roast came out. There must have been considerable organisation about our kitchen in those days. However, there certainly was always a cake of some sort, because after we'd slept off the effects of that great midday Sunday meal, there had to be afternoon tea. And what's afternoon tea without a home-made cake? The joy of Daisy was that you didn't have to worry about icing it, which was always a nuisance when you'd finished everything else to have to start on that. In her book my mother has written across the top of her recipe "This

♥ ♥

cake is a novelty, as it comes from the oven iced and finished". Why it was called Daisy Cake I'm not at all sure, except that it gives a nice yellow and white effect which might have reminded some imaginative soul of the big yellow-centred white daisies we grew in our garden. It is a good moist cake, and keeps well.

- ♥ ½ cup butter
- ♥ ½ cup sugar
- ♥ 2 eggs
- ♥ 1 cup SR flour
- ♥ 3 tablespoons milk
- ♥ ½ teaspoon vanilla
- ♥ grated rind of an orange and a squeeze of the juice
- ♥ 1 extra tablespoon sugar for topping
- ♥ ½ cup desiccated coconut

Beat the butter and sugar together, and then the yolks of the eggs. Add the flour and the milk, vanilla, rind and juice, and beat well. Put into a greased tin. Beat the whites of the eggs to a stiff froth. Add 1 tablespoon of sugar and beat again. Then add desiccated coconut. Spread this mixture over the top of the cake batter, and bake in a moderate oven for ¾ hour.

BANANA CAKE

Mother sent me this recipe when I first went to live in Sydney. Later when she came to stay with me, she enquired if I ever made it. Yes, I did, often. "And what sort of icing do you find best with it?" she asked. In those days, your father worked at home, sitting up in the little turret studio, tapping away so hard at his typewriter that he scarcely saw the whole blue Sydney Harbour spread out before his windows, and it was not always easy to get him away for meals. However, when I baked that banana cake, the sweet, crisp smell of it, wafted gently up the stairs and hovered enticingly over the typewriter, and ...

"Mother", I said. 'I've never had time to ice it.
We always eat it hot."

- ♥ ¼ lb. butter
- ♥ 1 cup sugar
- ♥ 2 eggs
- ♥ 2 large bananas, mashed
- ♥ 1½ cups SR flour
- ♥ ½ teaspoon carb. soda
- ♥ 2 tablespoons warm milk

Cream the butter and sugar, and beat in the eggs. Add mashed bananas, and then flour and carb. soda dissolved in the milk. Bake for about ½ hour in a moderate oven. It is, of course, meant to be cooled and iced, and mother herself always used a slightly lemony icing.

REG'S DUNDEE CAKE

Dundee is such a classic that I don't suppose there is anything different between this recipe and any other, except that for me this brings back such good memories. Reg was the dear friend who took up cooking after his wife's death and whose Quiche Lorraine I have already given you. He was a meticulous cook, as you can see. His Dundee Cake never fails.

- ♥ 10 oz. plain flour
- ♥ 4 oz. mixed candied peel
- ♥ 4 oz. sultanas
- ♥ 2 oz. angelica
- ♥ 2 oz. crystallised ginger
- ♥ 4 oz. glacé cherries
- ♥ rind of 1 lemon
- ♥ 8 oz. butter
- ♥ 8 oz. caster sugar
- ♥ 5 eggs 1 tablespoon brandy
- ♥ $3/4$ teaspoon carb. soda dissolved in 1 teaspoon milk
- ♥ 3 oz. ground almonds
- ♥ pinch salt
- ♥ 2 oz. whole blanched almonds

Sift the flour. Chop the peel and fruit. Split the whole almonds. Grate the lemon rind. Beat the butter to a cream and gradually beat in the sugar. Mix the flour with the chopped fruit. Add the eggs and floured fruit to the creamed butter and sugar, alternately, a little at a time, beating well. Add the brandy and carb. soda dissolved in milk, ground almonds and salt. The mixture should be rather stiff. A little extra milk may be useful if the eggs are small. Turn into a tin which has been greased and lined with grease-proof paper. Smooth the top with a palette knife and cover the surface with the split almonds. Bake at 350°F until cooked and the almonds are browned, about $2^{1}/2$ hours.

NEVER FAIL CAKE

Here's another one that never fails. And what's more it says so, for that's the only name I've ever known it by. Kate and I first tasted this sitting by the side of a road in Ontario, Canada, picnicking on our way to visit the Stratford Shakespearian Festival. Ruth, who was driving us, not the New York Ruth, but another equally good cook, had been up at the crack of dawn to bake it before we started out, so that it was still very fresh when we ate it. After the first mouthful Kate and I, almost in one breath, asked for the recipe. Since then, we've made it many times. In many different places. Kate used to say, "The minute we get into a new kitchen, Mummy makes a Never Fail Cake". Perhaps it was a subconscious hope for the future. It is frequently, and unaccountably different, but it has always lived up to its name. It never fails, and it is always delicious.

- ♥ 1/2 cup butter
- ♥ 1 cup sugar
- ♥ 2 eggs
- ♥ 1 teaspoon vanilla
- ♥ 1 cup sour cream
- ♥ 2 cups flour
- ♥ 1 teaspoon baking powder
- ♥ 1 teaspoon carb. soda
- ♥ 1/2 teaspoon salt
- ♥ 1/2 cup raisins

FOR THE TOPPING, MIX TOGETHER:

- ♥ 1/2 cup chopped nuts
- ♥ 1/4 cup sugar
- ♥ 1 teaspoon cinnamon
- ♥ 1/4 cup raisins

Cream butter and sugar. Add eggs and continue beating. Fold in the vanilla and sour cream. Stir in flour, baking powder, carb. soda and salt, sifted together. Add the raisins.

Grease a ring tin, and put in half the batter. Sprinkle this with half the topping, and cover with remaining batter. Sprinkle with the rest of the topping. Bake in a 350°F oven for 45 to 60 minutes.

BOB'S CAKE

During the Second World War, when Australian husbands were overseas for long stretches of time, we who sat at home not only knitted, but also baked cakes. We baked them in round "Soldier's Tins" which were bought for the purpose, sewed them up in unbleached calico, wrote numbers and those seemingly meaningless military addresses on them in big black letters, carried them to the post office, and handed them over with faith. Into the cakes went plenty of our precious and hard to get butter and eggs for they had to keep, since who knew where they were going or when they would get there. Also, of course, love and hope and a great many thoughts which couldn't be put in words and sent in letters. This is what went in to my Soldier's Tin.

- ♥ 1/2 lb. butter
- ♥ 1/2 lb. sugar
- ♥ 4 eggs
- ♥ 10 oz. flour
- ♥ 1 teaspoon cream of tartar
- ♥ 1/2 teaspoon carb. soda
- ♥ 1/2 lb. currants
- ♥ 1/4 lb. sultanas or raisins
- ♥ a little lemon peel
- ♥ a few almonds
- ♥ 1/4 cup rum

Beat the butter and sugar to a cream, add the eggs and beat well. Sift the flour with cream of tartar and carb. soda. Then add them, alternately with the mixed fruit and almonds. Add the rum last. Line a tin with greased brown paper and cook in a slow oven for 2 hours.

MY SISTER'S LOVE CAKE

Not *my* sister, of course, but a good friend just the same, for here's an addition to the collection I wouldn't be without. It came one Christmas all the way from Malaysia with a note saying "The YWCA believes in sharing resources, so here's my sister's recipe for Love Cake. It's good".

- ♥ 8 oz. butter
- ♥ 10 oz. sugar
- ♥ 6 eggs, separated
- ♥ 8 oz. finely chopped cashew nuts
- ♥ 8 oz. semolina
- ♥ ½ teaspoon baking powder
- ♥ essence of rose
- ♥ 1 teaspoon vanilla essence
- ♥ 1 teaspoon grated nutmeg
- ♥ 2 tablespoons honey

Cream the butter and sugar. Add the egg yolks, one at a time, and beat well. Fold in cashew nuts, semolina and baking powder. Add essence of rose and vanilla, grated nutmeg and honey. Mix well. Lastly fold in the beaten egg whites. Pour into a flat tin lined with grease-proof paper and bake in a moderate oven till the top is golden brown and the cake set, ¾ to 1 hour.

MRS SHEW'S ORANGE CAKE

Mrs Shew was a friend of my aunt's. She lived at the beach which was one of the reasons I liked to be taken to visit her. She was also a very good cook, renowned for this cake and two different kinds of cookies all of which found their way very quickly into our hearts and our cookbooks.

- ♥ ½ cup butter
- ♥ ½ cup sugar
- ♥ 1 egg
- ♥ grated rind and juice of 1 orange
- ♥ 2 cups SR flour
- ♥ 1 teaspoon baking powder dissolved in a cup of sour milk
- ♥ 1 lb. chopped dates
- ♥ ½ cup icing sugar

Cream the butter and sugar, add the egg, and the grated rind of the orange. Stir in the SR flour, and then the baking powder and sour milk. Lastly, add the dates. Bake for 1 hour in a moderate oven. Pour over the strained juice of the orange mixed with the icing sugar immediately after you have removed the cake from the oven.

BETTY'S BLOW~AWAY SPONGE

It's impossible to give you cake recipes without including at least one sponge. We made these so often – the higher the better – light as a feather – or at least that was the way we always hoped they'd be. Sometimes they weren't. Sponge cakes can be temperamental. But they had the same advantage as Daisy Cake. Once they were cooked, you didn't have too much to do with them. A spread of apricot jam and plenty of whipped cream in their middle, and a sprinkling of icing sugar on top and there you were. This particular recipe came to me from one of the "Battalion Wives" during the war.

- ♥ 4 eggs, separated
- ♥ 1 small cup caster sugar
- ♥ 1 dessertspoon coffee essence
- ♥ ³/₄ cup cornflour
- ♥ 2 large teaspoons plain flour
- ♥ 1 teaspoon cream of tartar
- ♥ ¹/₂ teaspoon carb. soda

Beat the egg whites until stiff. Add the sugar. Beat the yolks separately, and add coffee essence. Mix into the whites. Fold gently in the cornflour, flour, cream of tartar and carb. soda (previously mixed) and bake in a rather cool oven for about 15 minutes.

THE COOKIE JAR

In my memory, the cookie jar was always full. Of course, I really should say the biscuit tins, for "cookie" is a word I acquired in America, and anyway there was more than just a jar in our pantry. As I remember it there were always several tins full. There *was* a jar. One of those big glass, screw topped ones in which you found boiled sweets and humbugs at the corner store. It stood on the shelf just inside the pantry where we children could reach it, and on our return from school we were allowed to take two of whatever was there. Mostly they were rock buns. My father made rock buns sometimes, but the recipe I remember most is

PEARL'S TASMANIAN ROCKS

Another one of those recipes from my mother's Tasmanian childhood. Perhaps she, also, ate Pearl's Rocks when she came home from school. We certainly did.

- 1 lb. flour
- 1 teaspoon cream of tartar
- 1 teaspoon carb. soda
- 1/4 lb. butter
- 1/2 lb. sugar
- 1 cup currants or sultanas
- 1 egg
- a little milk

Sift the flour, cream of tartar and carb. soda together, and rub into it the butter and sugar. Add the currants. Beat the egg and milk and stir into the flour to make a stiff dough. Drop in teaspoonfuls onto a greased tray and bake in a moderate oven.

NUTTIES

These were another we often found in the "after school" jar. They were not usually for visitors, though I am not sure why, because they were very good.

2 cups rolled oats
♥ 1 cup flour
♥ 1 cup sugar
♥ a pinch salt

♥ ¼ lb. butter
♥ 1 tablespoon treacle
♥ 1 level teaspoon carb. soda

Mix together oats, flour, sugar and salt. Melt the butter and treacle in 2 tablespoons of boiling water, stir in the carb. soda and mix with the dry ingredients. Put small spoonfuls on a greased tray and bake in a moderate oven. Be careful. They burn easily.

But mostly biscuits were made to be served to guests – with the cup of morning coffee, with afternoon tea or for supper. Sometimes they were very fancy, sometimes plain and good "keepers". But they were always there. It was a very sad day indeed if all the biscuit tins were empty.

MRS SHEW'S WALNUT BISCUITS

Here's the first of Mrs Shew's famous cookies. They were for visitors, though of course we had some too.

Mix 1 cup SR flour with 1 dessertspoon of sugar. Rub into this 1 cup of butter, and press the mixture into a flat cookie tin.

For the topping:
- ♥ 1 cup walnuts
- ♥ 1/2 cup desiccated coconut
- ♥ 2 cups brown sugar
- ♥ 1 teaspoon vanilla
- ♥ 1/4 teaspoon salt
- ♥ 2 tablespoon flour
- ♥ 1/2 teaspoon baking powder
- ♥ 2 eggs

Chop the walnuts and mix all the dry ingredients well. Add the beaten eggs and vanilla and spread evenly on top of the first mixture. Bake in a moderate oven for about 20 minutes. When cool cut into fingers and ice with a butter icing.

CHINESE CHEWS

The second of Mrs Shew's biscuits – and our favourite.

- ♥ 2 eggs
- ♥ 1 1/2 cups dark brown sugar
- ♥ 1 cup chopped dates
- ♥ 1 cup chopped walnuts
- ♥ enough SR flour to make a not-too-stiff dough
- ♥ 1/2 teaspoon baking powder
- ♥ icing sugar

Maybe good cooks are always vague as to directions. Apart from listing the ingredients Mrs Shew contents herself with saying "do not cook too much". My own method is to beat the eggs and the sugar, add the dates and walnuts and then approximately a cup of SR flour sifted with the baking powder. Put the mixture into a buttered, flattish tin and cook for about 20 minutes in a moderate oven. Cut while hot into fingers, and roll them in icing sugar.

WINSOME'S BISCUITS

At one point, during the War, I worked in the advertising section of a department store. The world of department stores has always fascinated me and I enjoyed every minute of it, and made many friends, from the manager of groceries who chewed coffee beans, to the girl in cosmetics who told me to put a little eye shadow on my lids and fade gently upwards – an instruction I've often wished I could follow. And then there was the girl in the art department who sat, long legged and beautiful, on her stool and sucked her paint brush. We were always telling her it would make her ill, but she continued to sit, placidly sucking and glowing with vitality, long after I left the office. Her name, appropriately enough, was Winsome, and as well as looking decorative, she could cook. She used to bring these cookies to eat between mouthfuls of paint.

- ♥ 1 egg
- ♥ 3/4 cup sugar
- ♥ 1 cup peanuts (not chopped)
- ♥ 1 1/4 cups SR flour
- ♥ 1 large dessertspoon cocoa
- ♥ 1/2 teaspoon salt
- ♥ 1 teaspoon vanilla
- ♥ 1/4 lb. butter

Beat the egg and sugar well. Add the nuts, flour, cocoa, salt, vanilla and sugar and beat well again. Lastly add the melted butter. Put in spoonfuls on an oven tray and bake about 10 minutes in a moderate oven. Leave on trays to cool.

CARAMEL BISCUITS

Although these are not strictly biscuits, they were always considered as such. This particular recipe was one my aunt made, though I must admit it is a recipe I have come across in several different countries. With small variations perhaps, but obviously the same thing.

- ♥ ¹/₄ lb. butter
- ♥ ³/₄ cup sugar
- ♥ 1 egg
- ♥ 1 teaspoon vanilla
- ♥ 1 cup dates
- ♥ ¹/₂ cup walnuts
- ♥ 1 cup SR flour

Melt the butter and sugar in a saucepan to boiling point, then add the beaten egg, vanilla, dates and walnuts, and lastly the flour. Bake in a sandwich tin for 20 minutes and cut into slices.

MRS BRETT'S PEANUT BISCUITS

Mrs Brett appears often in my aunt's cookbook. I didn't know her, but she was obviously a friend of long standing, since her recipes keep popping up throughout the book. They are all good.

- ♥ ¹/₄ lb. butter
- ♥ ¹/₂ cup sugar
- ♥ 1 egg
- ♥ 1 cup SR flour
- ♥ pinch salt
- ♥ 1 cup chopped peanuts

Cream the butter and sugar, add the beaten egg, flour, salt and peanuts. Drop in teaspoons on a well greased tray and cook in a moderate oven.

HIDDEN DATES

My job in that advertising department was to do a daily radio session. At the radio station was a girl called Tommy whose mother would send us parcels of these cookies to eat with our morning coffee.

Needless to say, I asked for the recipe.

Rub ¼ lb. butter into 8 oz. flour, ½ cup coconut and ½ cup sugar. Mix to a dough with 1 beaten egg. Pinch off small pieces of dough, and roll a date in the centre of each piece. Roll in coconut and bake in a moderate oven for 15 to 20 minutes.

MRS OSWALD'S CORNFLAKE COOKIES

Mrs Oswald was a friend of my mother's, and it amuses me to see her recipe written into the book so formally. She was a close friend for as long as I can remember, and she and Mother saw each other frequently. Yet neither of them ever got round to using Christian names. They did get round to recipe exchanging though.

- ♥ 4 oz. butter
- ♥ ¾ cup sugar
- ♥ 1 egg
- ♥ 1½ cups SR flour
- ♥ ½ cup of walnuts
- ♥ cornflakes

Beat the butter and sugar to a cream, and add beaten egg. Then mix in flour and nuts. Roll small pieces of mixture in cornflakes and bake in a moderate oven on a greased slide.

The following two recipes were among my mother's favourites. They are good to eat, of course, but I think now that what really endeared them to her was that they were fairly inexpensive, made a large quantity, and kept well.

RICE BUBBLE BISCUITS

It seems likely we may originally have found this on a breakfast cereal packet, though to be honest, I don't remember we had packet cereals much. It was more, "Eat up your good oatmeal porridge, dear, that's what gives the little Scotch girls such lovely rosy cheeks". It was one of the first biscuit recipes I ever learned to make, and I was not nearly as fond of them as my mother. For having learned, it seemed as if it was forever being required of me. It was the great standby for school picnics, church fêtes or anything else where it was convenient to make a lot at a time.

- ❤ 1/4 lb. butter
- ❤ 1 scant cup sugar
- ❤ 1 egg
- ❤ 1 heaped cup SR flour
- ❤ 4 cups rice bubbles

Now I come to look at those quantities I don't think it can have come from a packet. They don't go in for scant anything as a rule. Cream the butter and sugar, add the beaten egg, then flour and rice bubbles. Put spoonfuls on a greased tray and bake in a moderate oven. They will spread a bit, so not too close.

GINGER CREAMS

- ½ lb. shortening
- 1 cup sugar
- 1 egg
- 1 tablespoon golden syrup
- 2½ cups SR flour
- 1 teaspoon carb. soda
- 1 tablespoon ground ginger

Mother always used good beef dripping for these biscuits. Half a pound of butter would have greatly reduced their appeal in her eyes. You can also use margarine. Cream the shortening and sugar and add the beaten egg. Stir in the golden syrup, then add flour sifted with carb. soda and ginger. Put small teaspoons on a slide and cook in a moderate oven. These can be joined together with a creamy mixture of butter, icing sugar and a little lemon, but we always had them plain, despite the fact we still called them "creams".

GOLDEN CRUNCHES

Long after we were grown up and married, Mother acquired another golden syrup biscuit. I don't know where the recipe came from, but it is simple and delicious. Every time I went home, there would be a tin of them somewhere in the kitchen, and even when she was old and found cooking a chore, this was a recipe she continued to make. In an air tight tin they will keep crisp and good for a long time.

- ♥ 2 tablespoons milk
- ♥ 1 level teaspoon carb. soda
- ♥ 1 dessertspoon golden syrup
- ♥ 1/4 lb. butter
- ♥ 1/4 lb. white sugar
- ♥ 1 cup SR flour

Heat the milk with the carb. soda and the golden syrup. Beat the butter and sugar until creamy and add the hot liquid. Stir in the sifted flour. Drop teaspoonfuls on to a shallow greased tray, allowing space for the biscuits to spread. Bake in a moderate oven for 10 to 12 minutes. While still hot, lift them off the tray and onto a rack to cool.

BURNT BUTTER BISCUITS

This was one of my own contributions to the cookie jar. Over the years people have pointed out that the name is not very attractive and that it's psychologically bad to call anything "burnt". However, that's the name under which they came to me, and that's how I pass them on to you. I've never had any trouble getting people to eat them.

- ♥ ½ lb. butter
- ♥ ½ lb. sugar
- ♥ 1 egg
- ♥ ½ lb. SR flour
- ♥ pinch salt
- ♥ blanched almonds

Melt the butter in a small saucepan and cook gently until it turns caramel coloured. Leave to cool. When cold, add sugar and beat to a cream. Add the egg and beat again. Stir in the flour and salt sifted together, and mix well. Roll into small balls and press a piece of blanched almond on top of each. Cook in a moderate oven until golden brown.

YO-YO BISCUITS

Both my mother and my aunt have this in their books as "Margaret's biscuits" because I was the one who actually brought it into the family. It is strange how full of biscuit and cake recipes are those old handwritten books, while mine has hardly any. And those I do have are the old ones, from my childhood and early married years. Do people not like cookies any more? Or do we not have time any longer for the finicky business of baking them? Yo-yo biscuits are worth the effort.

- 6 oz. butter
- 2 oz. caster sugar
- 6 oz. plain flour
- pinch salt
- 2 oz. custard powder

Beat the butter until soft and then cream it with the sugar. Slowly work in the flour, salt and custard powder. Take small quantities and roll into balls. Place on a slightly greased slide and press each one flat with a fork. Cook for 15 minutes and put together with raspberry jam, or a mixture of butter, icing sugar and vanilla.

MRS LONGBOTTOM'S SHORTBREAD

Because my mother made this recipe for as long as I can remember, it never seemed to me to be a funny name. It was simply what shortbread ought to be called. It's what shortbread ought to taste like too. Good.

- 9 oz. SR flour
- 3 oz. ground rice
- 3 oz. caster sugar
- 6 oz. butter

Mix the first three ingredients and rub butter into them. Press into a dry dish and cook in a slow oven about 3/4 hour. Cut into shape while hot. Mother always used a round sandwich cake tin for hers, pressing the dough with her knuckles, and pricking it here and there with a fork. When cooked, she cut it into wedge-shaped pieces.

BAILEY BISCUITS

Although it was Mother Bailey who gave me this recipe, it was Bailey children who always made it. And I think it is likely that the grandchildren Baileys are now producing it in several countries. It is the sort of simple recipe children like to make, and everybody likes to eat.

- ♥ 6 oz. SR flour
- ♥ 3 oz. brown sugar
- ♥ 2 oz. cornflakes
- ♥ 1 oz. cocoa
- ♥ pinch salt
- ♥ 6 oz. butter

Mix all dry ingredients together. Melt the butter and pour over. Drop in spoonfuls on greased slide and cook in a moderate oven. When cold, ice with chocolate icing. And don't try eating them before icing. They need that extra sweetness on top.

Noelle was my mother's cousin, renowned among other things for being the owner of a cat called Mrs Edwards. It was one of Mrs Edward's kittens that Kate once offered to Vivien Leigh, whom we met on a plane going from Honolulu to Australia. Miss Leigh wrote a charming letter explaining that much as she loved cats, and much as she'd like to have a kitten belonging to a cat called Mrs Edwards it was difficult to take with her on tour. But in my mind, Noelle is connected with quite a different animal ...

HEDGEHOGS

Goodness knows why they are called that, but they are – or were – a great Australian institution, and everyone had their own variety. The basic recipe, delicious just the way it is, comes from my mother.

Put into a saucepan 4 oz. butter and 4 oz. sugar and heat until they are melted. Add 1 well-beaten egg and 2 tablespoons cocoa. Boil until it thickens, stirring all the time. Take off the fire and add 6 oz. broken coffee or marie biscuits, and a cup of chopped nuts. Put into a tin lined with grease-proof paper and allow to set. Cut into squares. My aunt liked to add chopped ginger to hers, and some people put in raisins. You can also ice them with plain, thin white icing and scatter a few finely chopped nuts over the top. Noelle's recipe is fancier – but at heart it is still a hedgehog.

- 4 oz. melted butter
- $1/4$ cup white sugar
- 1 tablespoon cocoa
- 1 beaten egg
- $1/2$ lb. marie biscuits
- 1 cup coconut
- $1/4$ cup walnuts, chopped

Melt the butter, sugar and cocoa over hot water. Remove from heat and add beaten egg, then the other ingredients. Press into a greased Swiss roll tin and allow to set.

Topping: Mix 2 cups of icing sugar, 1 level tablespoon custard powder, $1/4$ cup butter and 2 tablespoons boiling water. Stir over hot water, pour over biscuit mixture and leave to set.

Icing: Melt 3 oz. cooking chocolate with 1 good tablespoon butter over boiling water and pour over biscuits. Cut into squares when all is set.

GINGER AND APRICOT SLICE

Biscuits which didn't have to be rolled or dropped, but could simply be cooked in one flat sheet and then cut up afterwards, were always a joy. It saved so much trouble. This is a particularly good one.

- 4 oz. butter
- 3/4 cup sugar
- 1 egg
- 2 oz. chopped nuts
- 2 oz. preserved ginger
- 3 oz. dried apricots (soaked in boiling water for 30 minutes)
- 1 1/2 cup SR flour
- pinch of salt
- 1 tablespoon cocoa
- 1/4 teaspoon cinnamon
- 1/2 cup milk

Cream the butter and sugar, add the egg and beat well. Add the nuts, ginger and apricots, chopped. Sift the flour with salt, cocoa and cinnamon, and fold in alternately with the milk. Spread in a greased Swiss roll tin and bake for 25 to 30 minutes in a moderate oven. Turn out and when cold, ice with chocolate icing and chopped nuts. Cut in squares.

PART SIX
other things to do

AT THE BACK OF THE OLD RECIPE
BOOKS THERE WAS ALWAYS A CHAPTER
CALLED "MISCELLANEOUS", "ODDS AND
ENDS", OR SOMETIMES MORE LOGICALLY
"HOUSEHOLD HINTS". IT WAS FULL OF
FASCINATING THINGS LIKE "HOW TO
MAKE A SILVER CLOTH", "THE BEST WAY
TO CLEAN FIRE IRONS AND FENDERS"
AND "PASTILLES FOR PRESERVING MEAT
BY FUMIGATION".

EVEN MY MOTHER'S AND MY AUNT'S BOOKS HAVE, SANDWICHED IN BETWEEN MRS LONGBOTTOM'S SHORTBREAD AND PEARL'S ROCKS, RECIPES "FOR RHEUMATISM", "FOR CORNS", "FURNITURE POLISH" AND "A GOOD TONIC" ($1/2$ QUART BOTTLE PORT WINE, 1 LARGE BOTTLE STOUT, $1/2$ TIN MALT EXTRACT, 2 OZ. BOVRIL). However, even I, who love the old kitchen ways so much, see no sense in passing on to you things which can surely now be better bought in shops, so my odds and ends chapter is strictly of the edible variety. I do realise that jams and pickles may also be better bought in shops, but it is a pity to lose all these old recipes and sometimes it is good to be able to produce your own. Not always economic, of course, if you don't have the fruit growing in your garden, but pots of home-made jams make excellent gifts. It is interesting, how much everyone loves the "home-made" variety even when it is really not as good as the mass-produced kind. I wonder if it brings back to everyone the big sunny kitchens of their youth, the assembly lines of children and aunts, who chopped and weighed and stirred, the big copper pans bubbling on the stove and the warm sweet smell of hot jam. And oh, that heavenly ritual of putting a few drops from the long-handled spoon onto a plate, standing it in the open window to cool, tipping it up to see if it "ran in folds" and being allowed to scrape it off the plate and taste it afterwards.

MRS JONES' STRAWBERRY JAM

When I was a child, we always had strawberries growing and consequently we always made strawberry jam. My mother had a great reputation for her strawberry jam, and I can vouch for the fact that it was always especially good. The recipe, as you see, came from Mrs Jones – the same Mrs "Oodnadatta" Jones who gave us the cream puffs.

- ♥ 12 lb. strawberries
- ♥ 1¹/₂ lb. sugar each lb. of fruit

As soon as fruit boils, add sugar and let boil for 3 minutes. Then add 3 dessertspoons of tartaric acid and boil again quickly for 5 minutes. Tie down the next day.

MRS DARK'S FIG JAM

We had a fig tree too, so fig jam was another standby. I don't know who Mrs Dark was, but I feel as if I do, for I have known her fig jam all my life.

- ♥ 6 lb. figs
- ♥ ¹/₄ teaspoons salt
- ♥ juice of 2 lemons
- ♥ ¹/₂ lb. preserved ginger
- ♥ ¹/₄ cup vinegar
- ♥ 4¹/₂ lb. sugar

Cut up figs and barely cover with water, then boil for 1 hour. Add the rest of the ingredients, and boil until it sets. To check if it has set, put small spoonfuls on a plate, let it cool, then tip it to see if it is thickened. When it has, that's the moment to take it off.

AUNT ETHEL'S FIG PRESERVE

The way I liked figs best, though – other than straight off the tree and slightly warmed by the sun – was in this recipe, given to my mother by that same friend from the Oodnadatta days who was known to us all as "Aunt Ethel". There were always several jars of this on the cellar shelves and if we were lucky, we had it over our blanc mange. It was too special, however, to be dished out with a very liberal hand, and consequently we loved it all the more.

- ♥ 8 lb. sugar
- ♥ 2 cups light vinegar
- ♥ 12 lb. figs

Boil the sugar and vinegar in 1 cup of water for 15 minutes, then drop in the whole figs and boil for 2 hours without stirring. Not even once. Mother always added whole blanched almonds and sliced ginger. Her recipe gives no indication at what stage she did this, but I suggest just before you pour the whole thing into jars and seal it up. My memory is of a fairly strong taste of ginger and the almonds white and crisp. But add according to your taste. You can use either stem or crystallised ginger.

MOCK GINGER

I must always have been fond of ginger, because this was another favourite. I loved its sharp crispness against the bland background of blanc mange or custard with which it usually appeared on our table. I once thought to make this in America but could not find anyone, anywhere who knew what a piemelon was or where I could find one.

Nor did I have any success in explaining about the limewater. It is something that appears often enough in old recipes, and was used (as I know to my cost) medicinally – at least by some people in some cases. The very elderly, and not to be gainsaid, mother of a friend of mine once absolutely insisted on my drinking some to prevent the sickness of pregnancy. The result was immediate, embarrassing and not preventive! However, in mock ginger I can assure you it has only good results.

It is ordinary slack lime which is used.

Cut 12 lb. piemelon into $1/2$ inch cubes, and stand them in limewater overnight. My mother adds "$3/4$ lb. lime is enough to cover the melon". She doesn't say how much water. Obviously we are supposed to know. I have taken my cue from another recipe in another of her books and use $1^1/2$ gallons of water to $3/4$ lb. of lime. You need enough to cover the melon. Add the lime to the water and let it stand and consider itself for 10 minutes. Then strain and pour over the melon.

Next day put 12 lb. of sugar into 1 gallon of water and let it boil for 5 minutes. Drain the melon and add it to the syrup.

According to my mother, you then "throw in" $3/4$ lb. of dry ginger which you have previously bruised, put into a muslin bag and soaked all night. There is a certain careless gaiety which I liked about that instruction to throw in something you have so carefully treated and clothed in muslin, but frankly I find it easier and more decorous simply to add $1/2$ lb. of preserved ginger cut into small pieces. Add the juice of 5 or 6 lemons to the melon, syrup and ginger and boil all together for 3 to 4 hours. Add a little more water if it seems to be boiling too dry.

THREE-DAY MARMALADE

Not the quickest recipe you've ever come across but, I think, the best. I used to make it in New York to give away for Christmas gifts, and it was much appreciated, but never tasted as good as when my mother made it. Perhaps nothing ever does. In the days of instant everything, I find it rather restful to attempt something which, while not difficult, takes three days to make.

Take 1 orange and 1 lemon, and slice them thinly. To each cup of sliced fruit, add 3 cups of water and let it stand until next day. Then, boil rapidly for 10 minutes, and again leave it until the following day. Finally, on the third day, measure what you have in your pan, and for every cup of pulp add 1 cup of sugar. Let it boil until tests show it is done.

There were many marmalade recipes in our family, but this was the one my mother always made, and I find it a good one because starting with 1 orange and 1 lemon never seems quite so frightening as facing up to the enormous quantities of fruit many recipes call for. Of course you can always cut things down to size according to your family and your kitchen, but all the same ... However, as I say, there *are* other recipes. After her Mildura holiday for instance, my aunt brought back this one.

MILDURA MARMALADE

1 large grapefruit, 1 orange, 1 lemon and 1 small pineapple. Shred
all finely and put in pan with 10 cups of water. Stand overnight.
(No, no, my dears, you can go to bed, it's the fruit I'm talking
about.) Next day, boil the mixture slowly until reduced by half –
about an hour. Then add, 1½ cups of sugar to each cup of pulp
and boil until it sets.

CITRON PRESERVE

Despite its large quantities, I cannot resist including this one, because
it is so good. I am sure my mother cut it down considerably, for she
made it each year with fruit given her by a friend and she certainly
never had 12 lb. of it. I always thought of it as Mother's very own recipe
because she was so fond of it, and I have never known anybody else
who made it. However, in searching for her way of doing it, I discover
the recipe came originally from the *Green and Gold Cookbook*, so I
offer them my grateful thanks for one of the most delicious preserves
I know, and commend it to you.

Boil 12 lb. of citrons in plenty of water until they are soft. Then
take them out of the water and when cool, cut into square pieces
and remove the pulp and pips. Put 18 lb. of sugar and 8 pints of
water into a pan and boil for 20 minutes. Add the peel, and the
pulp, carefully strained. Boil for 1½ hours.

❤ ❤

PRESERVED CUMQUATS

Another thing that was found in our cellar from time to time was preserved cumquats. My mother had two recipes for this, carefully recorded in her book. One I can hardly forbear from giving you because it not only suggests "throwing" six dozen cumquats into the syrup after you have pricked them with a long hat pin, but also advises that "a large washhand jug is the best receptacle" to soak them in. But the recipe I give is the one my mother really used, and the one I also have followed, without recourse to either hat pins or washhand jugs. If you make this amount, however, you will need a very large something to soak them in, and a washhand jug would be very useful if you happened to have one around some place.

- ❤ 6 lb. cumquats
- ❤ 6 lb. sugar

❤ ❤

♥ ♥

Have your cumquats with a very small piece of stalk still attached, and prick them well with a silver fruit fork. (Well that's better than a long hat pin, but if you don't happen to have one try a thick darning needle or a skewer.) Soak them in cold water for 1 hour, then change the water, put into a pan and bring to the boil. In a separate pan, have your 6 cups of sugar and 2 cups of water boiling. As soon as the cumquats reach boiling point, snatch them off the flame, drain them and add them to the boiling syrup. Careful. They break easily. Let them almost come to the boil, but take the pan off the fire before they actually do so. Let them stand all night and the next day carefully take the cumquats out of the syrup again. Once more, bring the syrup to the boil, put back the cumquats, and once more whip them off the heat before they actually boil. Let them sit peacefully all night again, and repeat the process next day. They must never really boil or you will toughen the skins. After this third cooking, bottle them, putting a good spoonful of brandy on top of each before sealing it down.

♥ ♥

We had a very large cellar in our house. It was necessary, not only because we had no refrigerator, but also because – well, where else would you store all those jams, jellies, pickles and preserves? Of course, there was the pantry but that was where we kept the cakes and biscuits, the big bins of sugar and flour (cheaper to buy in quantity, of course) and the groceries. Always one packet unopened in the pantry and one in use in the kitchen, was the rule. Good housewives didn't run out of the necessities. Oh how often I have wished for space like that, as I stood in my modern kitchen – smaller than my mother's pantry – and surveyed the lovely built-in cupboards, so carefully arranged above my reach, and not one of them big enough to hold a proper preserving pan. Our pantry shelves easily held the largest of the earthenware mixing bowls, the big round pan in which mother cooked her jam and a certain quantity of the jam itself. When the jars were opened they were transferred to the tall, two-storeyed safe, which stood in the kitchen, its feet in containers of water to frustrate the ever-hopeful ants, and its sides made of fine wire mesh to let the breeze in and keep the flies out. There were hazards to be faced even in those spacious kitchens. There was a safe in the cellar too, which hung from the ceiling and in which we kept the meat. But the greatest joy of the cellar were those wide wooden shelves with their rows of bottled fruit, and their brown stone jars of pickles. There was something very satisfying about that sight. One felt one could withstand a siege if necessary. There were all shapes and sizes of jars. And all colours. The big yellow peaches, the small purple plums. The reds and oranges of jams and jellies. The fat brown figs. But what I remember most, is the bright mustard yellow of the cauliflower pickle.

CAULIFLOWER PICKLE

- ♥ 3 lb. cauliflower
- ♥ 3 onions
- ♥ salt
- ♥ 2 quarts vinegar
- ♥ 1 tablespoon turmeric
- ♥ 1 teaspoon mixed spice
- ♥ 1 teaspoon curry powder
- ♥ 1 cup sugar
- ♥ 4 tablespoons flour
- ♥ 3 tablespoons mustard

Cut up the cauliflower and the onions and cover with boiling water into which you have put a handful of salt. Allow it to stand overnight, then drain and throw away the water. Heat the vinegar in a saucepan. Mix all the other ingredients to a smooth paste and add to the vinegar – careful now, no lumps please. Then add the cauliflower and onions and boil gently until tender.

If you live by the rule of a roast on Sunday and cold meat on Monday, (and who didn't?) then you need a good deal in the pickle and chutney line to go with it. Both my mother's and my aunt's books are full of such recipes. I offer you only three, neither of them difficult, and both good. The first is an old one coming, I think, from the Tasmanian days, for it is written in both their books in a slanted, elderly handwriting which didn't belong to either of them. I wonder if it was Pearl's.

TOMATO RELISH

- ♥ 12 large ripe tomatoes
- ♥ 4 large onions
- ♥ 1 lb. sugar
- ♥ 1/2 tablespoon mustard
- ♥ 1 tablespoon curry powder
- ♥ vinegar
- ♥ 1 small handful salt
- ♥ 5 chillies (can be omitted if wished)
- ♥ cayenne pepper to taste

Cut the tomatoes and onions to the size of walnuts, sprinkle with salt and let them stand over night. In the morning, drain off the liquid and boil the tomatoes and onions for 5 minutes with sugar and enough vinegar to cover. Add the rest of the ingredients and boil for 1 hour. Bottle when cold.

TOMATO SAUCE FOR IMMEDIATE USE

Here's a quick and useful one, given me by the same E.S. Cutlack who provided our Christmas Tomato Pie. In these days, when if you are lucky enough to own a cellar, it isn't always as well stocked as it used to be, this is a useful recipe to have.

You'll need tomatoes and equal their bulk in onions. Also pepper, salt, sugar, butter and breadcrumbs. Cut the tomatoes roughly and grate or chop finely the onions. Cook over a slow flame for about 1/2 hour and then rub through a strainer. Add seasonings to taste, a little butter, salt, pepper and sugar. (Personally I've always thought a touch of basil might be an improvement.) Then add enough fresh breadcrumbs to thicken well. E.S. Cutlack says firmly "It must not be sloppy". Very good, he adds, with mutton either hot or cold.

PEACH CHUTNEY

We had peaches growing in the garden so this was not as difficult for my mother to make as it has always been for me. However, if you can get the peaches, it is an excellent chutney, very good in sandwiches and savouries as well as with cold meat.

Take 5 lb. of yellow peaches, and cut them up, without removing the skin. Mince 1 lb. seedless raisins, ½ lb. onions, and ½ lb. preserved ginger. Put this, together with the peaches, 5 lb. sugar, ½ oz. cayenne pepper and salt to taste into a saucepan and boil until it thickens like jam. Take off the fire, and when it has stopped bubbling but is still hot, add 1 quart of vinegar. Let it stand for 48 hours before bottling it. Taste it and add a little more vinegar if you think it is necessary.

PICKLED WALNUTS

One early summer day in France, not long ago, I was walking down a tree-lined avenue with my good cooking friends, Marjorie and Basil. Marjorie and I had our eyes fixed on the little round, fairy-tale turrets of the chateau we were about to visit, but Basil looked at the spreading branches overhead, and the springing turf beneath our feet. He bent to pick up a walnut, still snugly and shinily clad in its bright green skin. "Just right for pickling", he said. And without thinking I replied, "About December 20 and always before New Year's Day". Then I remembered I was in the wrong country and on the wrong side of the equator. *My* recipe for pickled walnuts was meant for the gnarled old tree in my aunt's Melbourne garden. It is a recipe my brother makes, not I. I must admit that I have always bought my pickled walnuts in a jar, but who knows? One day you, too, may live in a house with a walnut tree. Aunt's recipe says:

About December 20, and always before New Year's Day. Prick the walnuts with a fork. Put them in an earthenware bowl and cover with brine (using about 2 oz. salt to 3 pints water). Leave for 3 days.

Drain, rinse, and repeat the process, so that the walnuts are in brine three times. Then spread them out to dry for 3 days. They should go black. For the vinegar mixture, use $1/2$ gallon vinegar, and 1 oz. each of cloves, peppercorns, whole spice, whole ginger (bruised) and 3 lb. sugar. Heat this in a saucepan, and when it is hot put in the walnuts. Simmer them until they are soft and swelled out. Test them with a fork, and when done, put in a crock (oh, for those brown, earthenware crocks of my childhood!) and cover with liquid.

This, according to my aunt, makes half a bucketful.

TUTTI FRUTTI

If there is a real recipe for this, I don't know it. The only time I tried to make it according to somebody's rule, it turned out badly, so since then I've gone by instinct, the way I happened to be feeling and where I was. We didn't have it in my childhood, though I can't think why. We had the fruit available, the large stone jar to put it in, and the cool dark cellar for storing. But somehow it's one good thing we missed out on completely, and it seems ironic that when it would have been so easy I didn't know about it and since it has been so much more difficult I have made it regularly. Maybe I like the challenge.

The principle is simple. Into a large stone jar, with a lid, put about 2 pints of good brandy, and add to it, layer by layer, all the soft fruits of summer as they come into season. First the strawberries, then the cherries (stoned, of course), the peaches, raspberries and apricots. As you add them, also add sugar, approximately $1^1/2$ cups to each cup of fruit. Black currants are good, and I like a few gooseberries, but no apples, pears or grapes. One year I added walnuts as an experiment and they were good. (Except one night I served it to someone who was hideously allergic to walnuts. Oh dear! It needs frequent gentle stirring with a long wooden spoon, much earnest consideration and much tasting. Keep it in a cool place for at least 3 months before using.

ORANGE DRINK

As well as the jams and pickles and chutneys, there were also bottles of drink in our cellar, for although you could buy fruit syrup of various kinds, it was considered cheaper and better for you to make your own. There were always bottles of ginger beer, made in some mysterious way from a "plant" and which had to be fed and divided and rebottled. And unless you drank a good deal of it you began to feel like the sorcerer's apprentice with bottles of ginger beer multiplying all around you. Aunt has a recipe for Pearl's ginger beer, which begins with the impossible instruction "Take 4 dippers of cold water". And there was a sweet lemon syrup which almost everybody's mother made. But the one I liked best was an orange drink which was always on hand and very good. It's also very simple to make.

- ♥ finely grated rind and juice of 6 oranges
- ♥ 5 lb. sugar
- ♥ 2 oz. tartaric crystals
- ♥ 1 oz. citric acid
- ♥ 1 oz. epsom salts
- ♥ 3 pints boiling water

Stir all well until dissolved, and bottle.

❤ ❤

HELEN'S BARLEY DRINK

Whenever we were ill, mother made barley water for us, but it was not this recipe. My mother had her own. This is, however, the recipe that Helen gave me early in my married life and that I then made during the famous lemon barley water episode in India. It began one day when we were living at Maidens Hotel in Old Delhi, and I discovered one of our number sitting in her room gazing gloomily at a tin of Robinson's Barley. When asked what was the matter, she said the doctor had told her to drink barley water and she'd obediently bought the barley but now found she'd no idea what to do with it. "I'll make it for you", I said, and carried the tin and a lot of lemons – which are very small in India and take forever to squeeze on a strange sort of ball-and-cup wooden squeezer – back to my room to unearth Helen's recipe. In due course I produced lemon barley water which my friend adored. Even her husband said it was the best thing he knew – with a spot of gin in it. Actually, he's not the only one who feels this way about it. Although the recipe will forever be "Helen's" to me, it came – I was about to say "originally", but who knows what the origin of any recipe is – from her friends Gwen and Suzanne whose mother apparently made it daily. Now they – in company with that Delhi husband – find it one of the best mixers ever. "Gin and barley water?" their guests

❤ ❤

❤ ❤

say. Then they taste it and quickly come back for more. But to return to Maidens Hotel. The little group of us living there at that time were very close. The wives, in fact, were known as the Maiden Mothers, because we sat about under the trees together sewing and gossiping like a Mother's Club. So pretty soon, my lemon barley water had been tasted by all, and one after another friends would come to the door with their empty bottles saying, "If I buy the lemons and the barley, will you make me some of that marvellous drink?" In the end I was spending my whole day squeezing lemons and the whole of Maidens Hotel must have been awash with Helen's barley drink. I don't think the bearers will ever forget the performance, and I am not at all sure that they believed it was only barley water I was putting into those empty gin bottles. I don't suppose it will ever taste as good as it did on those hot Indian afternoons, but it is a recipe that brings back memories and I cannot bear it to be lost.

- ❤ 7 pints of water
- ❤ 5 tablespoons pearl barley

Boil 20 minutes, strain and add sugar and lemon juice to taste.

❤ ❤

The last of my Other Things take us up out of the cellar and into the kitchen or perhaps even into the drawing room. The first is

MRS FRENCH'S RAISIN LOAF

This friend of my mother's was a favourite for many reasons. One was that she was the only person I ever knew who used an ear trumpet which is pretty fascinating to a child. The only trouble was that she didn't use it long enough, for she was a forward-thinking woman, and way back in my childhood she changed it for an almost equal fascinating little box which she sat on the table in front of her and turned on when she wanted to hear you. And before long, she was using quite an ordinary modern hearing aid which didn't appeal to us at all. She had bright laughing eyes, and a mobile, laughing face. She was also a good cook, but although I remember several of her recipes my mother made, this was the only one I found written down.

- ♥ 1 cup sugar
- ♥ 1 cup seeded raisins
- ♥ 1 small teaspoon carb. soda
- ♥ 1 tablespoon butter
- ♥ 2 cups SR flour
- ♥ pinch of salt
- ♥ 1 egg

Put 1 cup of water, sugar, fruit, carb. soda and butter into a pan, and stir until melting. Then add the flour, salt and beaten egg. Bake in a loaf tin in a moderate oven for about 3/4 hour. Serve sliced and buttered.

TREACLE LOAF

Another very similar slice-and-butter tea-time loaf is this which came to me from a very different source in another country and some

30 years later but obviously with a shared ancestry. It is easy to make, and oh so easy to eat.

PLACE IN A MIXING BOWL IN THIS ORDER:

- ♥ ¹/₂ cup sugar
- ♥ ¹/₂ teaspoon mixed spice
- ♥ ¹/₂ teaspoon carb. soda
- ♥ 1 dessertspoon butter
- ♥ 1 tablespoon treacle

Add ¹/₂ cup boiling water and when all ingredients are melted and mixed add 1¹/₂ cups of plain flour. Mix well, and pour into a greased loaf tin and bake in a moderate oven 25 to 30 minutes.

PUFFTALOONS

We used to have these for tea on cold, wet Sunday afternoons and they were delicious. Sometimes we called them fried scones but that's a plebeian name for them, and in any case the only recipe for fried scones I have ever found turned out to be a breakfast dish and served with bacon. Pufftaloons were light and crisp, and you sat around the fire and split them open, putting a piece of butter in the centre and maybe a little golden syrup. Then you licked your fingers and asked for more. How we managed to eat them on top of our normal Sunday dinner I do not know, and why we weren't all overweight is an equal mystery.

- ♥ 8 oz. SR flour
- ♥ ¹/₂ teaspoon salt
- ♥ enough milk to make a light dough – about ¹/₂ cup

Roll out about ½ inch thick, and cut into squares. Fry in deep fat till well puffed and golden brown. Drain on paper before serving.

A much more elegant recipe which my mother sent me when we were in New York is

POCKET BOOK ROLLS

New York is not the place for fancy afternoon teas. At least, not the kind of New York I knew. We did get invited periodically to official teas by the Australian Office of Information of course and one elderly Anglophile we knew served both Chinese and Indian tea daily in her elegant 79th Street penthouse – along with small thin sandwiches and chocolate biscuits. But in our house, everyone worked, and the only thing which could possibly come under the heading of Tea was probably Kate's after-school peanut butter and jelly sandwich. Since this was a situation my mother wouldn't have understood – there were weekends of course when we *could* have been civilised and had tea but didn't – I didn't tell her I never made her recipe. I pass it on to you, though, because she did make it, and I did eat it with her. It is as good as she says. I give it to you exactly as my mother gave it to me.

Rub 2 oz. of butter into 8 oz. SR flour. Moisten to a nice dough, with about 1/2 cup of milk and water. Roll out until 1/4 inch thick. Cut into circles with a 3 inch fluted cutter, put a few flakes of butter into the centre of each circle, and moisten the edge halfway round with milk. Fold dough over the butter and press the edges lightly together. Stab a skewer in four times at intervals, round the sealed edge 1/4 to 1/2 inch in from the rim. Bake in a hot oven on an ungreased tray for about 12 minutes. They look charming little pastries. Slip a little butter and a slice of cheese between the folds and pack with lettuce, celery and/or apple. They are best eaten warm and are lovely buttered for afternoon tea.

SELF~RAISING FLOUR

So many Australian recipes call for self-raising flour and I have so often been in countries where it is either unobtainable or difficult to find that I feel I should tell you how to make it. I discovered this recipe in my mother's cookbook and have always found it worked very well.

- ♥ 3 lb. flour
- ♥ 1 oz. cream of tartar
- ♥ 1/2 oz. carb. soda
- ♥ 1 teaspoon salt

Mix all well together with the hands, sift twice through your flour sifter and store for future use.

PART SEVEN
high days and holidays

SOME RECIPES ARE THE ALL-THE-
YEAR-ROUND KIND. OTHERS HAVE
THEIR OWN TIMES AND SEASONS,
EACH BRINGING WITH THEM SPECIAL
MEMORIES AND NOSTALGIA. MANY
ARE CONNECTED WITH THE CHRISTIAN
YEAR, FOR GOOD CHRISTIANS HAVE
ALWAYS KNOWN THAT FOOD WAS A
GIFT OF GOD, TO BE ACCEPTED WITH
GRATITUDE AND ENJOYED.

♥ ♥

I LIKE THE STORY OF ST TERESA OF AVILA WHO WAS HAPPILY EATING A PARTRIDGE WHEN SHE WAS CONFRONTED BY A VERY DISAPPROVING LADY WHO OBVIOUSLY THOUGHT SAINTS SHOULD BE ABOVE SUCH THINGS. ST TERESA REMARKED, "THERE IS A TIME FOR PENANCE AND A TIME FOR PARTRIDGE" AND, VERY SENSIBLY, WENT ON EATING. And long, long ago, I read somewhere – and of course it's the sort of thing I never forget – that if you serve your spinach with a good lacing of butter and garlic you are following a very good example indeed, for it is known as the Virgin Mary's Spinach.

But all that is by the way. Let's get back to some of those recipes which, in our not-very-saint-like family, have been associated with our times of celebration.

The high days of childhood, of course, were birthdays, and a birthday cake then was always a Rainbow Cake. A good butter sponge – probably Emma's Sandwich – made in three layers, one white, one chocolate, and one coloured pink with cochineal. And, oh, you had to be so careful not to make it a bright, unseemly red by being too heavy-handed with the colouring. My mother managed by dipping a matchstick first into the cochineal bottle and then into the cake batter, mixing after each dip until she got the shade she wanted. She was very particular about it. I think the three layers were considered quite carnival enough for children, and a butter sponge better for their digestions than some, but as we got older we demanded fancier things. Rich, dark chocolate cakes, and confections of whipped cream. We weren't so interested in our digestions, that's obvious – nor in our weight.

My most vivid recollection of a birthday cake is one I once made for Frances, not as a little girl easily pleased with a simple "Rainbow", but as a young lady with quite sophisticated tastes. She decided to have herself a birthday party and asked if I'd contribute a chocolate cake of which she was particularly fond. Flattered, I said "Yes" before asking how many guests were expected. A foolish oversight, for in the end I had to make two cakes, which was quite something. This is not the simplest cake to make, nor the cheapest, but one of the best – rich and moist and good to eat, and very impressive to look upon.

♥ ♥

FRANCES' CHOCOLATE BIRTHDAY CAKE

- ♥ 1 dessertspoon instant coffee
- ♥ 8 oz. semi-sweet chocolate
- ♥ 8 eggs
- ♥ 1 cup sugar
- ♥ 1 cup plain flour

First mix the instant coffee with 1 cup of boiling water and set aside.

Preheat the oven to 350°F and grease two 9-inch cake tins, lining the bottom with grease-proof paper. This is a delicate cake which will stick or break easily if the tin is not well greased or you forget the wax paper.

Add the chocolate to $1/2$ cup of the coffee (you'll need the rest for the filling later on) and melt it over hot water. Let it cool slightly while you beat together the eggs and sugar until they are very thick and pale yellow in colour. Then fold in the flour and the chocolate. Don't skimp on the beating, for there is nothing else in the recipe which makes the cake rise. Pour the batter into the prepared tins and bake for about 35 minutes, or until the cake tests done. Despite your best beating, it is not a very high-rising cake, but you'll find this is adequately compensated by the filling and topping which is thick and rich. The cake itself should be light, but not very high. When you take it from the oven, let it wait a minute or two before turning it onto a rack to cool. It is never a good idea to up-end cakes the minute they come from the oven. They like a moment to settle. When the layers are quite cold, spread the following mixture between them and over the top and sides.

- 4 egg yolks
- 1 cup sugar
- $1/4$ teaspoon cream of tartar
- 5 oz. semi-sweet chocolate
- $1/4$ cup of the coffee left from the cake
- 6 oz. butter
- 2 tablespoons rum

Beat the egg yolks until light and fluffy. In a small pan, combine the sugar and cream of tartar and $1/3$ cup of water, and bring to the boil, stirring until the sugar is dissolved. Then boil rapidly until the syrup spins a thread, or registers 236°F on a candy thermometer.

Gradually beat the syrup into the egg yolks and continue beating until the mixture thickens. Put the chocolate into the ¼ cup of coffee and melt it over hot water. Stir this into the egg mixture. Then beat in the butter, a little at a time, mix in the rum and chill the cream until it is a spreadable consistency.

When you have covered your cake – top, centre and sides – with this delicious concoction, any leftover cream can be put into a star-tube and piped on top for decoration or for holding the birthday candles. Then, as a final touch, press flat chocolate discs all round the sides of the cake, edge to edge, like a crown.

To make the chocolate discs: melt 8 oz. of semi-sweet chocolate over hot but not boiling water until it is smooth. On a sheet of wax paper, mark 24 circles about $2^{1}/2$ inches in diameter and spread a thin, even layer of the melted chocolate over each circle. Place on a cookie sheet and chill until firm. Remove the wax paper and put the discs around the cake.

You can easily see why it is wise to enquire the number of guests before starting out on this one. More than 16, and my advice to you is – don't.

Quite the biggest cake I ever made was Kate's wedding cake. Luckily it was one of those rare occasions on which I read the recipe right through from beginning to end and made my plans accordingly. I am renowned for starting cooking before really reading the recipe – a habit which has caused me quite some bother from time to time. In the case of Kate's wedding cake, it would have been fatal. But at the time I was a very busy lady with a weekly script schedule to meet and even I knew that the only way I could cope was to get organised and to work systematically.

The first thing I realised was that all my mixing bowls were too small. So someone kindly lent me one of those big old hand basins such as used to stand on a cedar table in my grandmother's bedroom, and in it I did the mixing. With my hands. I was wedding cake to the elbows, but it was the only way.

KATE'S WEDDING CAKE

This is not a cake you'll make very often. Weddings don't happen every day. But it is a recipe I hope will stay in the family, for it is indeed worth all the trouble it takes. But remember, its most essential ingredient is organisation. You have to make your plans well in advance and then work steadily through the different steps. I can't stress this too much.

Begin with the tins. It is a two-tier cake, and I used square tins, one 11 and the other 7 inch. They both need to be well greased and lined with three or four thicknesses of greased brown paper. It's a long, slow cooking and you must protect your cake from burning or cooking too hard around the edges. Then prepare the fruit.

- 6 lb. raisins
- 3 lb. sultanas
- 2¼ lb. currants
- 12 oz. mixed peel
- 6 glacé apricots
- 3 slices of glacé pineapple
- 6 tablespoons rum
- 6 tablespoons brandy

Wash and dry the raisins, sultanas and currants. Chop the peel and the glacé fruit. Put them all into a bowl and pour over the rum and brandy. Cover and let them stand until the next day, when it's time to mix the batter.

- 3 teaspoons mixed spice
- 2 teaspoons salt
- 2½ teaspoons baking powder
- 2¼ lb. flour
- 1½ lb. butter
- 1½ lb. brown sugar
- 12 eggs
- 12 oz. chopped blanched almonds
- grated rind of 3 lemons
- 2 tablespoons rum
- 2 tablespoons brandy

Measure and sift together the dry ingredients and use a little to dust over the mixed fruit and almonds. It prevents them from all going to the bottom. Cream the butter and brown sugar well, until light, and beat in the eggs one at a time. After the sixth egg, stir in a little of the flour mix to prevent curdling, and then – still one by one – beat in the remaining eggs.

Finally, add the rest of the flour alternately with the fruit and the almonds. Mix thoroughly. Do it with your hands and pray the phone won't ring or your nose start itching. Fill in tins carefully, so there are no empty spaces round the edge, and smooth the top with the back of a spoon.

Bake the larger cake in a slow oven for 8 hours. Cover the smaller one with aluminium foil and put it into the refrigerator until the next day. Then cook it in a slow oven for $3^1/2$ hours. It is wise to take it out of the refrigerator at least an hour before cooking.

As soon as the cakes come out of the oven, dribble over them a tablespoon each of rum and brandy. When they are quite cold, carefully remove their protective brown papers and wrap them first in foil and then in a tea towel. Store them in airtight containers until you are ready for the next step, which is the icing. To prepare for this first paint each layer with cake glaze.

- 4 tablespoons sugar
- 1 tablespoon glucose
- 1 tablespoon glycerine

Put the above ingredients into a saucepan with 2 tablespoons of water over low heat and beat until melted. Allow to cool and then brush all over the cake.

Over this goes the almond icing.

- 2 lb. sifted icing sugar
- 1 lb. ground almonds
- 4 egg yolks
- 4 tablespoons sherry

Mix the icing sugar and almond meal and add the beaten egg yolks and sherry to make a dough. Turn out onto a board dusted with icing sugar to prevent sticking, and knead until smooth. Divide the dough, and keep the smaller piece covered to prevent cracking.

Roll out the larger piece to about $1/2$ inch thickness and lift it onto the larger cake with your rolling pin. Then use the rolling pin to roll it over the top of the cake and over the sides, and the palms of your hands to press it down onto the sides so they are completely covered. A glass rolled around the sides of the cake will finish the smoothing process. A dusting of icing sugar on rolling pin, palms and glass will prevent sticking. Do the same with the smaller cake. And leave them for several days to allow the icing to dry.

At the end of this time, make the second coat of icing. I must admit I don't like icing cakes as a rule, but I did enjoy making this one. There is something very satisfactory about seeing it come out like a smooth, white blanket over your cake, and besides it goes by the absolutely splendid name of Super Cream Plastic Fondant.

- 4 oz. liquid glucose
- 1 lb. crystal sugar
- 5 oz. water
- 1 oz. glycerine
- 4–4$^{1}/_{2}$ lb. pure icing sugar
- 1 teaspoon cream of tartar
- 1 oz. gelatine
- 5 oz. water
- 4 oz. copha

Stir the first five ingredients over heat until sugar and glucose are dissolved. Bring to the boil and cook until the mixture forms a soft ball when dropped into a glass of cold water or registers 240°F on a candy thermometer. (If you are going to make fancy icings and desserts, a candy thermometer is a most useful piece of equipment. While it is fun to drop bits of this and that into cold water or to see if your syrup spins a thread, a thermometer is more accurate.)

Dissolve the gelatine in 5 oz. of water and add this to the glucose mixture. Add the chopped copha. Allow to cool and gradually beat in 2$^{1}/_{2}$ lb. sifted pure icing sugar. Place all this in a plastic bag and leave it for at least 24 hours, or longer if that suits you.

until a plastic consistency is reached. You can test for this by pinching a piece of the fondant between finger and thumb very thinly. When it holds its shape, then the consistency is right. Work in colouring if you want it and a few drops of vanilla. Roll out the amount you need to cover the larger cake. Keep the rest in a plastic bag until you are ready for it. Lift the rolled out icing carefully onto the cake with the rolling pin, as you did for the almond icing, and smooth it down the sides with your hands, this time dusted with cornflour to prevent sticking, until it covers the whole of the cake and is quite smooth. Cover the second cake in the same way and leave them for two more days.

Then, cut a piece of aluminium foil the same size as the smaller cake and centre it on the larger one. Place the smaller cake on top of the foil. This means that when you are ready to remove the second tier in order to cut the bottom one, it will lift off easily and leave the icing firm and smooth underneath. Secure the two tiers together by piping small icing rosettes all around the join. Pipe similar ones along the edges of both tiers. You will have to make a small amount of ordinary royal icing for this – the Super Cream Plastic Fondant is not meant for decoration. Finally, arrange a small bunch of garden fresh flowers and ribbon on top, and your cake is finished.

The Tuesday before Lent, as everyone knows, is Shrove Tuesday, and when we lived in New York this was the day that St Bartholomew's Church traditionally served pancakes. They were made by a line of young men, sitting on stools at a long table, with tall cook's hats on their heads and bowls, pans and electric hotplates before them. With great expertise they sat and tossed off pancakes all evening, until the batter bowls were empty and the customers full. It was great fun, and I expect a good money-raiser for the church, too. Those, as I remember, were the flat American pancakes served with butter, maple syrup and crisp pork sausages, but at least one of those young men also knew about the thinner rolled-up kind which, for me at least, is the true Shrove Tuesday pancake. His recipe is not so very different from my own, but he gave it to me saying that it was an old family one, and that his mother's grandmother had made it every Shrove Tuesday "back in the Old Country". That's the sort of build-up I never can resist, so here it is.

STEPHEN'S SHROVE TUESDAY PANCAKES

- ♥ 2 eggs
- ♥ 1½ cups milk
- ♥ 1 cup flour
- ♥ ½ teaspoon salt
- ♥ grated rind of 1 lemon, and the juice of 2
- ♥ ½ cup sugar

Beat the eggs until light. Add the milk and beat some more. Add the flour, salt and lemon rind, and continue to beat. The batter should be thin. Pour into a lightly greased hot pan, tilting the pan so it will be covered as thinly as possible. Fry until bubbles come through the batter, then turn. When the pancake is lightly browned, turn out onto a warmed pastry board. (That's the kind of instruction I love!) Sprinkle with lemon juice and sugar, and roll the pancakes, putting them side by side on an oven-proof dish and keeping them warm in the oven while you cook the rest. Sprinkle some more sugar on to the rolled pancakes and burn it in several places with a three-pronged fork which has been made very hot over a flame. This recipe will make about fourteen 8 inch pancakes.

Once Shrove Tuesday is past, you don't have to put away your pancake pan. Pancakes, with the proper kind of filling, have always been considered good fare for meatless days. And even if you don't want to go completely meatless, they're still a useful addition to the menu. Here's one suggestion.

JOCK'S SPINACH PANCAKES

- ♥ 8 oz. cooked spinach, squeezed out but not too dry
- ♥ 8 oz. cottage cheese or cream cheese
- ♥ 2 large eggs
- ♥ pepper and salt
- ♥ 2 or 3 chicken livers

Put half the spinach into the blender with half the cheese and 1 egg, with a seasoning of salt and freshly ground pepper. (My recipe says ten grinds of pepper, but you don't have to count.) Blend, and then transfer to a basin. Do the same with the second half of the ingredients. Sauté the chicken livers in a little butter. Pepper and salt them, chop them up and add to the spinach mixture. Chill the mixture and use it to fill your pancakes. When filled, line them up neatly in a flat, oven-proof dish, and pour over some good tomato sauce. Top with grated parmesan cheese and heat in a 300°F oven for about half an hour.

To make the tomato sauce: Chop 2 onions and cook till soft in a generous amount of butter. Chop half a green pepper and cook for a few minutes with the onion. Peel 3 large tomatoes, cut them roughly and add to the onion and pepper. Season with black pepper, salt, a sprinkle of sugar, 2 cloves, a bay leaf and a little oregano. A little chopped garlic if you like it, and a dash of celery salt are also good additions. Partly cover, and let it cook very slowly, giving an occasional stir. When everything is cooked, soft and mushy, and you have a satisfactory consistency, taste for seasonings, rub through a sieve and spoon over your pancakes.

Part way through Lent, on the Fourth Sunday, comes Mothering Sunday, the day when we eat Simnel Cake, created so they say by the baker father of Lambert Simnel, a pretender to the throne in the reign of Henry VII. According to legend, he also finished up among the pots and pans, spending the last years of his life as scullion in the royal kitchens.

As with its cousin, the Christmas cake, there are many recipes for this spicy confection. Mine is a good one, though more complicated than some. Still, you only make it once a year after all. Bake it in the first weeks of Lent, and it will cut moist and mellow when the Fourth Sunday comes around.

SIMNEL CAKE

- 1 cup sultanas
- 1/2 cup seedless raisins
- 1 cup currants
- 1 cup chopped mixed candied fruit
- 2 cups flour
- 1/2 teaspoon nutmeg
- 1/4 teaspoon cinnamon
- 1/4 teaspoon ground cloves
- 1/4 teaspoon allspice
- 6 oz. shelled, blanched almonds
- 5 eggs
- 1 1/2 cups caster sugar
- 1/4 teaspoon almond essence
- 1 teaspoon baking powder
- 6 oz. butter

Line a deep 8 inch cake tin with two layers of greased brown paper, allowing the paper to stand up an inch above the top of the tin. Preheat oven to 300°F. Put the fruit into a basin. Mix 1 cup of the flour with the spices and sieve it over them, tossing the fruit so that it is well covered with the flour.

Grind the almonds. It is possible, and easier, to use almond meal, but better to grind your own. They are moister. Beat 1 egg. Reserve 1 tablespoon of the ground almonds and mix the rest with 1/2 cup of sugar, the almond essence and about half the beaten egg. Knead until the paste sticks together. Sprinkle a board with the reserved ground almonds and put your almond paste on it.

Pat it into a round exactly the same size as your cake tin, cover it with a cloth, and leave it while you make your cake.

Sieve the remaining cup of flour with the baking powder. Cream butter with the remaining cup of sugar until light and fluffy, then

beat in the 4 eggs one at a time. (I always add the half left over
from the almond paste, too. It seems a pity to waste it.) After the
second egg, mix in a little of the sieved flour to prevent curdling
and then add the remaining 2 eggs, beating after each one. Fold in
the rest of the flour and baking powder, and the floured fruit.

Spoon half the cake batter into the prepared tin, gently sit the
round of almond paste on top, and then spoon in the rest of the
batter. Cook for $2^{1}/2$ to 3 hours, until the cake tests done. Cool
on a rack. When cold, remove the brown paper, wrap in foil and
store in an airtight tin for at least a week before topping with
almond icing.

TO MAKE THE ALMOND ICING:
- ♥ $1^{1}/2$ cups blanched almonds
- ♥ $1/2$ cup caster sugar
- ♥ $1/4$ teaspoon almond
  essence
- ♥ 1 egg, lightly beaten
- ♥ 1 egg white

Grind the almonds and mix with the sugar, almond essence and
enough of the whole, beaten egg to make a stiff paste. Knead until
the paste sticks together.

Brush the top of the cake with the egg white and pat the almond
paste on top of the cake in a thick, even layer. Press a cake
rack on to it in two different directions to make a pattern, or
mark with the tines of a fork. Pinch around the edges to make
a piecrust-like frill. Bake for 5 to 10 minutes, until a few brown
spots begin to show around the edges. Allow to cool, and then put
back into the airtight tin until the Fourth Sunday comes around.

♥ ♥

EASTER BONNET PUDDING

Then comes Easter, and it just shows that childhood habits die hard when I can, unblushingly, state that our Easter speciality is known as Easter Bonnet Cake. Once you've made it, you realise why the Easter Bonnet part of the title – it looks like one – but "pudding" is definitely a misnomer for this light and airy dessert.

- ♥ 2 envelopes gelatine
- ♥ pinch salt
- ♥ 6 egg whites (you'll use the yolks in the sauce)
- ♥ $3/4$ cup sugar
- ♥ 2 cups whipping cream
- ♥ 1 teaspoon vanilla
- ♥ 1 cup flaked coconut

Soften the gelatine in $1/2$ cup cold water, then pour into this $1/3$ cup of boiling water and stir until it is quite dissolved. Add the salt to the egg whites and beat until they stand in peaks. Gradually, a little at a time, beat in the sugar, then fold in the dissolved gelatine.

Beat the cream till it is stiff, add the vanilla, and fold into the egg whites. Butter an 8 inch springform cake tin and sprinkle $2/3$ of the coconut on the bottom and sides, mostly on the bottom, I

♥ ♥

♥ ♥

think. Pour in the cream mixture and then sprinkle the remaining coconut on top. Leave overnight in the refrigerator.

Next day unmould it (on to a round flat white plate if possible, so it looks like the brim of your Easter bonnet. The colour doesn't really matter, but it should be round.) Decorate with a circle of fresh whole strawberries (if you can get them) or little white Easter daisies or ribbon around the bottom edge of your pudding – between the brim and the crown as it were. Serve it with a bowl of sliced, sweetened strawberries (frozen if fresh are unavailable) and the following rum sauce.

- ♥ 6 egg yolks
- ♥ 1 cup sugar
- ♥ 1/2 cup rum

Beat the yolks until thick and lemon coloured. Gradually beat in the sugar. Stir in half the rum and cook over boiling water, stirring all the time, until the sauce coats a wooden spoon. Don't let it boil. Stir in the rest of the rum and allow it to cool.

♥ ♥

"MY" PLUM TORTE

In Geneva, September brings us the Jeun Genevois, which was originally a day of prayer and fasting for those killed in the St Bartholomew's Day massacre. The fact that the Jeun Genevois comes several weeks after St Bartholomew's Day is indicative of the time it took the news to travel. They declared a day of fasting as soon as the news reached them. Why they should fast by eating delicious Tarté au Pruneau I simply do not know, but that's what tradition demands on the table on this particular day. I have the distinct feeling that it is all one is supposed to eat, but perhaps I am wrong about that. The real way to make Tarté au Pruneau is to use small purple, egg-shaped prune plums instead of apples. Cut them in half, or in quarters, depending on their size and the pattern you want to make with them. But I have another suggestion. It is by no means traditional, but then I am never truly convinced that we were intended to remember the martyrs with an orgy of plum tart. Anyway, my version is very good, and it makes a nice change in the autumn days when Geneva's market stalls are heaped so high with the little purple plums that it's almost wicked not to do something about them.

- 1 cup flour
- 1 teaspoon cinnamon
- 1/4 teaspoon salt
- 1 1/2 teaspoons baking powder
- 1/4 lb. butter
- 1/2 cup sugar
- 2 eggs, well beaten
- 1 tablespoon lemon juice
- 1/2 grated lemon rind

Sift the flour, cinnamon, salt and baking powder. Cream the butter and sugar until light and add the well-beaten eggs, beating the mixture until it is creamy. Add the lemon juice and rind, then stir in the flour mixture a little at a time.

Pour into a greased, flattish cake tin – 11 by 9 inch is the size I use – and press the stoned, halved plums into the batter, cut side up and close together. Over the top sprinkle ½ cup of sugar mixed with 1 teaspoon of cinnamon. Bake in a 350°F oven for 1 hour. Serve warm, and pass the whipped cream separately. If you're going to fast with plum tart, you might as well have whipped cream as well.

MÈRE ROYAUME SOUP

Another celebration which brings its own kitchen ritual to Geneva is the Fête of the Escalade which commemorates the victory of the Genevois over the Savoyards more than 350 years ago. On the night of December 11/12, 1602, the Duke of Savoy and his soldiers attempted to take the city of Geneva by stealth. With horses' hoofs muffled and under cover of darkness, they gathered outside the walls on Plainpalais (where now the flea market does a thriving trade on Saturday mornings and the circus lifts its coloured tents each summer). Silently, silently, they set up their specially made ladders and began their "escalade" – their ascent of those thick, high walls. Unfortunately for them, one good wife of Geneva was wide awake and in her kitchen stirring soup in her great iron pot, which is called a marmite. Above the friendly bubbling of her soup, she heard the soft, unfriendly sounds outside, and as the first luckless soldier struggled up his ladder, Mère Royaume tipped her soup over him – boiling liquid, bouncing vegetables, iron pot and all. No army could survive a shock like that first thing in the morning, could it? And while I understand that, historically, there is some doubt about the authenticity of this tale, the good Mère Royaume is still remembered in Geneva every December, and the chocolateries overflow with replicas of her famous marmite, filled to the top with brightly coloured marzipan vegetables. And every year it is the custom for the youngest Genevois in the house to smash the chocolate marmite with a clenched fist and the ringing words, "Ainsi perissent les ennemis de la Republique". (Thus perish the enemies of the Republic.)

I wish I could offer you Mère Royaume's authentic recipe for vegetable soup, but I guess nobody thought to ask her for it. It was a busy day, once she'd given the alarm, of course. However, this is the way I like to think she was going about it.

- 2 lb. beef soup bone with meat
- 1 veal knuckle
- 1 pig's foot
- 2 large onions
- 4 large tomatoes
- 2 bay leaves
- ½ cup uncooked rice or barley
- salt, peppercorns
- parsley
- 5 cups of assorted raw vegetables

Put all ingredients except the 5 cups of mixed vegetables and the rice (or barley) into a large saucepan with 3 pints of water and simmer slowly, covered of course, until the meat is tender and comes easily off the bones. Take the meat out, chop it into small pieces and set it aside. Put the bones back and continue to simmer. Altogether this should take about 2½ hours, and you will need to skim it occasionally during this time. Slice and chop the vegetables, and add them together with rice. Add more water if necessary. Instead of the rice you can use barley, lentils, dried beans – or a mixture of these things, but lentils and dried beans take longer to cook. Cook until the rice and the vegetables are cooked. Taste for seasoning, return the chopped meat to the soup and serve. Good vegetables to use are carrots, green beans, peas, potatoes, celery, cabbage, turnips. Use what is available and what you like. It is a recipe capable of great variety. You can leave out the pig's foot if you want to, or just use the beef bones, but all three make a very rich stock.

But there is more to the Escalade than nourishing vegetable soup.

It is also the time for Vin Chaud, that delicious hot wine that tastes so good and smells, as you brew it, almost better than it tastes. It warms our hands as well as our hearts as we cuddle our steaming cups and stand at a friendly window high above the Cour de St Pierre to watch the end of the annual Escalade procession. The windows are open, so noses and ears are chipping with cold. There is the snuffle and whinny of horses in the court below, the clear, sharp sound of hoofs on cobblestones and the clink and glitter of sword and halberd. People in the clothes of 1602 gather before the Cathedral, flickering in and out of the torchlight. There is no other light in the great square, normally so brightly lit with its floodlights on the Cathedral towers and the yellow squares of windows in the houses round about. Then the bonfire is lit. Flames rising high into the night sky, millions of tiny orange sparks dancing in the still cold air. And the singing begins. The voices of the Genevois, massed on the Cathedral steps, singing out their thanks for that long ago deliverance. We shut the windows and turn gratefully back into the warmth to pour ourselves another glass of Vin Chaud.

I got into the business of brewing Vin Chaud for the Escalade party quite by accident. There didn't seem to be anybody else to make it that year, and after all – I told myself – it really is only wine, water, sugar and spices. How can a girl go wrong? So, with a great deal of tasting and adding and general consideration all round, I produced what has become known as "Mrs Dunn's Instant Vin Chaud". It had to be instant, because I'd had no warning and there were a good many cold and thirsty people waiting. There are far more complicated ways of making it than this, and many more traditional recipes. I'm sure it should not be quite this instant. But so far nobody's refused to drink it, and most come back for a second (or a third) cup. And I've been making it now for a good many Escalade parties.

MRS DUNN'S INSTANT VIN CHAUD

- ♥ 3 lemons
- ♥ cloves
- ♥ 3 oranges
- ♥ 1 bottle of water
- ♥ 1$\frac{1}{2}$ cups sugar
- ♥ 3 sticks cinnamon
- ♥ 3 bottles of red wine

Peel the yellow skin from the lemons in long strips, and squeeze the juice from 1 lemon. Stick 4 cloves into each of the oranges. Measure the water in one of the wine bottles, or make a guess at it. Roughly a 1 to 3 ratio is what I like, but maybe when you've done a little tasting you'll want to alter this. Put oranges, peel, water, sugar and cinnamon sticks into a pan and bring to the boil. If you really have to be instant about it, cook until the sugar is melted and then add the wine and the lemon juice. But it is infinitely better if you can let the mixture simmer gently for 15 minutes, then add the wine and lemon juice and reheat. It should be hot, but don't let it boil again. Strain, taste and serve.

This is really very much a matter of taste and try. You may find you need more or less sugar, more or less lemon juice. It's up to you. As long as it fills your kitchen with a festive aroma, tastes good, and runs down the throat with a satisfying warmth, that's all you can ask.

THANKSGIVING PUMPKIN PIE

Although it's not as close to Christmas as the Escalade, the American pilgrim festival of Thanksgiving always seems to me to be too close for comfort. The cooking is much the same. You've no sooner finished one turkey dinner than you have to start cooking another. But there is one big difference. Thanksgiving brings us Pumpkin Pie.

- ♥ 2 eggs
- ♥ 1½ cups of cooked, mashed pumpkin (or tinned pumpkin puree)
- ♥ ¾ cup sugar
- ♥ pinch salt
- ♥ 1 teaspoon cinnamon
- ♥ ½ teaspoon ground ginger
- ♥ ¼ teaspoon nutmeg
- ♥ pinch of ground cloves
- ♥ ⅔-1 cups evaporated milk
- ♥ 1 x 9 inch unbaked pie shell

Heat the oven to 425°F.

Beat the eggs slightly, and add the pumpkin purée, mixing well. I find the tinned variety easier if it is available, but otherwise cook your pumpkin – the orange kind that we used to call ironbark – and purée it smoothly. Mix in the sugar, salt and the spices and stir in the evaporated milk. Taste, to be sure you've got the right blend of spices. You'll maybe like a little more nutmeg if you're as fond of it as I am. Then pour into your unbaked pie shell and cook for 15 minutes. Reduce the heat to 350° and continue cooking for another 45 minutes or until a silver knife comes out clean. Serve cold – with whipped cream if you want to be luxurious about it.

PART EIGHT
and oh, those Christmases!

AND OH HOW I REMEMBER THOSE
CHRISTMASES. FROM THOSE OF MY
CHILDHOOD WHEN WE ALTERNATED
BETWEEN MY AUNT NELLIE'S HOUSE AND
OUR OWN, TO THE FESTIVE ONES OF
NEW YORK CITY. I REMEMBER A CHILD'S
EXCITED CURIOSITY ABOUT PRESENTS,
WHICH WE KNEW WERE KEPT ON TOP
OF MY MOTHER'S CEDAR WARDROBE, BUT
COULDN'T ACTUALLY SEE. OF COURSE
THERE WERE SOME WHICH WERE NO
SURPRISE, BECAUSE WE GOT THEM
EVERY CHRISTMAS.

♥ ♥

THERE WAS ALWAYS AN ANNUAL FOR INSTANCE (*GIRLS' OWN*, *TIGER TIM'S*, *LITTLE DOT'S*) AND A MONEY BOX, A DIFFERENT SHAPE EACH YEAR, FOR SAVING UP TO BUY PRESENTS FOR THE FOLLOWING CHRISTMAS. I remember our first Christmas in Sydney when we sat up all night finishing a doll's house for Frances, so that the paint was still sticky, and we were still up, when she came creeping downstairs to the tree on Christmas morning. I remember the first cold Christmas in Larchmont, New York, and the splendid excitement of the white and snowy world. I remember the enormous turkeys and the fantastic present-wrapping which marked our New York City Christmases. And yes, most of all, I remember the cooking and the traditional dishes which were the stable ingredient of all our Christmases, producing another of those "crises de cuisines" which so fascinated Jean-Daniel.

As you grow older, as your familes grow, as you move about the world or settle down in one place, you will build up your own Christmas traditions. But here I give you, with love, the recipes which have gone towards making mine.

THAT MARVELLOUS TURKEY STUFFING

A little while ago I met up again with a friend who had spent Christmases with us in New York. We had not seen each other for a good ten years, but the minute I invited her once again for Christmas dinner, her first question was, "Do you still make that marvellous turkey stuffing?" Well, of course I do. Once made, never forgotten, and we've had it regularly with each Christmas turkey since 1955. It was given to me by a Greek friend in New York, but in fact came from an American in France, for it appeared first in one of the best cookbooks I know, *Clementine in the Kitchen*. It may have changed slightly since Clementine originated it, for it has passed through many hands on its way here (and I give it to you exactly as it came handwritten to me) but I still bow gratefully to her genius each time I make it. It is the best ever. And if there's any left over, try eating it on crackers with your Boxing Day aperitif.

Shell 2 quarts of chestnuts, bless you. Cook them till tender (bless them) in half water, half consommé, with 1 sliced onion, celery, salt and pepper. Let them get cold.

Meanwhile, chop 2 shallots fine and cook them in a little butter. Mix with 1/2 lb. sausage meat, 1 teaspoon minced parsley, some thyme, 3 sticks of chopped celery, 1/2 cup of brandy, 3 oz. canned truffles in Madeira wine (these can be replaced by a few mushrooms soaked in Madeira or sherry) and 1/2 cup breadcrumbs soaked in milk and well pressed out. Season to taste and mix with the now cold chestnuts. Stuff turkey. Cook turkey. Eat turkey. Love turkey.

GREEK TURKEY STUFFING

Oddly enough this recipe also came to me from a Greek friend. A different one, in a different country, and it is a very different recipe. It calls for a certain amount of imagination along with its ingredients, but it is good, and unusual, and sometimes you may like to vary your menu a little.

- ♥ 1 lb. chestnuts
- ♥ 1 large onion chopped
- ♥ 1 tea cup of rice
- ♥ 1 tea cup of currants or sultanas
- ♥ ³/₄ lb minced meat
- ♥ 1 coffee cup blanched almonds
- ♥ 1 teaspoon cinnamon
- ♥ salt and pepper to taste

Parboil the chestnuts and skin them. There should be a pound of them after skinning. Chop the onion and cook gently in a little water and a nut of butter. Add the chestnuts, with the meat, etc. and lastly the flavouring. Add just enough butter and water to prevent the mixture sticking to the pan. Cover, and let simmer for about an hour on a low flame.

"MY" CHRISTMAS CAKE

This is the Christmas cake I have been making yearly for … well I hate to say just how many years. But long before I was married. I give you the recipe, exactly as it came to me, but let us be honest, I have taken a good many liberties with it since I first tried it out. I use an extra egg for instance, and a greater variety of fruit, because I just happen to like both ginger and figs in my fruit cakes and sometimes pineapple too. And naturally, brandy. About ¾ cup in the cake itself, and when I take it out and while it is still hot, I pour a little extra carefully over the top just for good measure. There's no use being mean about these things at Christmas. However, just as it stands, the cake is very good and I leave it to you to try, and to use your imagination as you see fit.

- 1/2 lb. butter
- 1/2 lb. dark brown sugar
- 2 eggs
- 1 level teaspoon carb. soda
- 1/4 cup treacle
- 3/4 lb. plain flour
- 1/4 pint strong black coffee
- 1/2 lb. sultanas
- 1/2 lb. currants
- 1/4 lb. dates or figs
- 1/4 teaspoon ground cloves
- 1/4 teaspoon salt
- 1 tablespoon hot water
- 1/2 lb. raisins
- 1/4 lb. lemon peel
- 1/2 teaspoon mixed spice
- 1 teaspoon cinnamon
- 1/4 teaspoon nutmeg

Cream the butter and sugar. Add well-beaten eggs slowly. Dissolve the carb. soda in water and add to treacle. Sift the dry ingredients, then add alternately with the fruit, treacle and coffee, mixing well. Put into prepared tin and bake for 2½ to 3 hours, in a slow oven.

MRS HART'S CHRISTMAS CAKE

I suppose all Christmas recipes are fairly universal, and I have found variations of this recipe in other countries. My recipe was given me when I first married and went to Sydney, and I have used it ever since. I make it about a month before Christmas, wrap it in aluminium foil and store it in the refrigerator. It will keep 2 or 3 months there. To serve, I cut it in very thin slices.

- 1 1/2 cups shelled whole Brazil nuts
- 1 1/2 cups walnut halves
- 2/3 cups chopped candied orange peel
- 1/2 cup red cherries
- 1/2 cup seedless raisins
- 3/4 cup sugar
- 3/4 cup flour
- 1/2 teaspoon baking powder
- 1/2 teaspoon salt
- 3 eggs
- 1 teaspoon vanilla

Line a log cake tin with buttered paper.

Mix the nuts, fruit, flour, sugar, baking powder and salt, all well together. Beat the eggs and vanilla until light and fluffy and pour over the dry ingredients. Mix well. Spoon into the prepared tin and spread evenly. Bake in a very slow oven for 2 1/2 hours. Let the cake cool in the tin for at least 10 minutes before turning out.

MY CHRISTMAS PUDDING

I suppose everyone has their own recipe for Christmas pudding. This is mine. I have tried many but this is the one that I finally settled on as being the best. It is the one I have made every year since either of you can remember.

- 1/2 cup finely shredded beef suet
- 1/2 lb. plain flour
- 1/2 lb. brown sugar
- 1/4 lb. breadcrumbs
- 3/4 lb. sultanas (or 1/2 lb. sultanas and 1/4 lb. currants)
- 1 lb. seeded raisins
- 4 eggs
- 1 small teaspoon vanilla
- 2 tablespoons brandy
- 2 oz. chopped blanched almonds
- 1 teaspoon baking powder
- 1/2 nutmeg grated (or 1 level teaspoon grated nutmeg)
- salt

Rub the suet into the flour, then add the sugar and breadcrumbs, then the prepared fruits. Mix together the beaten eggs, vanilla and brandy, and add to dry ingredients. Mix well. Put in a floured cloth and boil 6 to 8 hours the first day, then 1 hour before serving. I like my Christmas pudding made with suet, but you can substitute 1/2 lb. of butter for the suet, if you prefer. In that case, cream the butter and sugar and add the eggs one at a time. Mix in the dry ingredients alternately with the brandy.

❤ ❤

RUTH'S MINCEMEAT

Nowadays, if I make mince pies, I always use this recipe. Ruth gave it to me in New York, and it was one of her family traditions. I have two theories about mince pie. One is that if you make it as one large pie, it should be served with plenty of whipped cream (if you're going to eat mince pie, you might as well forget about calories), and the second is that it's better to make small ones. In my childhood, one had small covered mince pies, and the tradition was that each one you ate guaranteed a happy month. The ideal was to eat 12, of course, but I never managed that. My way of making little mince pies is to cut identical-sized rounds of heavy aluminium foil and pastry. Fit the pastry over the foil and pinch up the edges five times, so you form a shallow star. Fill with a spoonful of mincemeat and bake. A dab of whipped cream on top just before serving adds to the merriment. The mincemeat I use, naturally, is Ruth's.

- ❤ ³/₄ lb. lean round steak, cut into strips like matchsticks
- ❤ 1¹/₂ cups finely chopped tart apples, peeled
- ❤ 1¹/₂ cups dark brown sugar

❤ ❤

- 1½ cups raisins and/or currants
- ¼ cup dark molasses (try treacle if you can't get molasses)
- ¼ cup chopped suet
- ½ cup chopped candied peel – orange, lemon, citron
- ½ teaspoon salt
- ½ teaspoon nutmeg
- 1 teaspoon cinnamon or to taste
- ½ teaspoon powdered cloves
- About ¾ cup cider and brandy combined

Simmer all together for about 1 hour. Let cool. More liquid can be added or it can be cooked longer to thicken more, until of the right consistency.

Ruth makes hers into one big round pie. She says: Line a pie dish with pastry and fill with mincemeat. Make a lattice of pie crust to cover top. Bake for about 40 minutes in a 400°F oven. Flambé with warm brandy.

THE CHRISTMAS COOKIE TRAY

Because your father's birthday was in December, he always celebrated with a great pre-Christmas party. Each year, as the time approached, we would tell each other that this year we could not afford to have that party as well as the normal festivities of Christmas Day itself. But each year we had it anyway. It was at one of these that the first Christmas Cookie Tray appeared and it has been a tradition in our house ever since.

There is no need to tell you, of course, that the weeks before Christmas were always occupied with a perfect fever of cookie making, so that by halfway through December every crock, tin and covered receptacle was filled with goodies for Christmas giving, and I was looking round vainly for a place to store the next batch. It was at this point that your father, seeing me sort of lost and helpless amid a sea of Santa Claus and Christmas stars asked reasonably, "Why don't we eat some, instead of putting them all away?" "They're for Christmas", I told him severely. "Well", he said, "we're having our Christmas party, let's put some on a tray and our guests can eat them". "Nobody wants cookies with cocktails", I pointed out. But he was a determined man, and in the end, our oblong silver tray, instead of occupying itself with drinks as usual, was filled with cookies, carefully arranged in rows and decorated here and there with a bit of tinsel, coloured ribbon and a silver ball or two. Thin fingers of Mrs Hart's Christmas cake went on it too. It did look nice. And as for not wanting cookies with cocktails ... we filled that tray three times before the last guest departed. Since then, no Christmas at our house has been complete without that special cookie tray.

What do I put on to it? Well of course it varies from year to year, depending where I am and how much time I have for cooking. I no longer make the dozens of Santa Claus, stars and trees that I did when I had so many young, willing and artistic hands to help decorate. But there are just one or two "specials" I always make no matter where I am, and without which no Christmas Cookie Tray is quite complete. They are not everybody's Christmas traditions – like liebkuchen or mincemeat bars – but they are mine.

CHOCOLATE WALNUT BALLS

- ♥ 4 oz. day-old sponge cake, crumbed
- ♥ 3 oz. unpeeled ground almonds
- ♥ 3 oz. caster sugar
- ♥ 1 tablespoon brandy
- ♥ 1½ tablespoons of apricot jam purée (made by heating 1 tablespoon of apricot jam with 1 tablespoon water and adding 3 teaspoons lemon juice)
- ♥ walnut halves
- ♥ chocolate icing

Mix the cake, almonds and sugar and add the brandy and purée. Roll the mixture into small balls, press a walnut half on top of each and reshape.

Put them on a flat tray and chill for 2 to 3 hours. Ice with chocolate icing and serve in small paper cups.

LUISE'S ALMOND CRESCENTS

- ¼ lb. butter
- 2 dessertspoons caster sugar
- ½ cup chopped blanched almonds
- 1 cup SR flour
- ¼ teaspoon salt

Mix the butter, sugar and almonds, then flour and salt and let stand for 1 hour. Take small pieces of the dough, form into rolls about 2 inch long and thick as your finger. Shape them into crescents, and cook in a moderate oven for 15 to 20 minutes. While hot, roll them carefully in caster sugar and cinnamon.

BUTTER BALLS

- ½ lb. butter
- ¼ cup sugar
- 1½ cups flour
- 1 teaspoon vanilla
- 1 cup walnuts, chopped finely

This is first cousin to Luise's almond crescents though it came to me on the other side of the world. It has its own distinctive flavour because of the walnuts and its final roll in sugar.

Cream the butter and sugar well, and mix in the flour, vanilla and chopped nuts. Form into small balls and cook in a moderate oven for approximately 30 minutes. Roll the balls immediately in icing sugar and set on a tray to cool. Careful not to burn your fingers. The hot sugar sticks to you as well as the biscuits if you don't look out.

WHITE CHRISTMAS

- ♥ 1 cup coconut
- ♥ 1 cup rice bubbles
- ♥ 1 cup icing sugar
- ♥ 1 cup powdered milk
- ♥ 1 packet mixed fruit
- ♥ 1 packet salted peanuts
- ♥ 1 packet cherries
- ♥ 1½ tablespoons sherry
- ♥ ½ lb. melted copha

Put the dry ingredients into a basin and mix well. Pour over them the sherry and melted copha and press into a flat tin. Allow to cool and set in the refrigerator and cut into squares. Best kept in the refrigerator too. This, as you can see, is really a recipe for making in Australia, because copha is, as far as I know, a strictly Australian thing. I find, however, that in other countries and under other names you can find pure coconut shortening which replaces it quite satisfactorily. As for those packets, I use 2 cups of mixed fruit, ¾ cup peanuts and ½ cup of cherries.

MRS TURNER'S OLD ENGLISH MINCEMEAT

This also is an old recipe, handed down and much travelled. Not as close to me in friendship as Ruth's, for Mrs Turner is one of those people whose recipes I use and am grateful for without ever having known her.

Her recipe was given to me by a French girl in Switzerland, so you see how these recipes get around. It is different from most mincemeats and very good.

- 8 oz. each of shredded suet, dried apricots, cooking apples, large prunes and sultanas
- 4 oz. each of glacé cherries, mixed peel and soft brown sugar
- 2 oz. almonds
- 1 teaspoon cinnamon
- 1/2 teaspoon ground cloves
- grated rind and juice of 1 lemon and 1 orange
- 1 tablespoon of syrup
- 1 pint ginger wine

Peel, core and chop apples, chop apricots, prunes, mixed peel, and almonds. Add cherries, sultanas, suet and spices. Add lemon and orange rind and juice, and syrup.

Stir all well together and then add the wine. Allow to stand 24 hours before bottling.

JOY'S CURRANT PIE

I am not sure how this recipe gets into this chapter. It is not a Christmas one. But, as with characters when one is writing fiction, so with recipes. They sometimes develop characters and wills of their own and will not be gainsaid. So this is not a Christmas recipe, but I feel it wants to be one. And why not? It has a good appearance, many of the right credentials and a charming flexibility that should commend it to any harassed Christmas hostess. It also has the added attraction of being not quite as richly sweet as most mince pies. So why not let it remain here among its Christmas cousins? Even its name has the right seasonal ring to it.

Several days beforehand put currants in a glass jar and cover with brandy. Line a dish with good, short crust. The size of it depends entirely on how many you plan to feed. You can use anything from a large oven tray to a small round pie plate, but it needs to be shallow. Cover the pastry with the drained currants to the depth of about half an inch – more if you like. Make the top white with a layer of sugar, then green with a good covering of chopped fresh mint, and then cover with pastry. Flute the edges together, prick the top with a fork and sprinkle on a little sugar. Cook in a fairly quick oven until the pastry is done. Remove from the oven and sprinkle a little more sugar over it. Serve warm with plenty of thick cream.

Joy, in giving me this recipe, said "you can't use too much mint", and I, taking her absolutely literally, have found that you can. However, the fact remains, it can take a lot of mint and exactly how much you personally like is something you must work out.

OLD FAVOURITE
CHRISTMAS SAUCE

In Australia, we always served our Christmas pudding with brandy sauce, a thin white sauce made with milk, cornflour, sugar and brandy, which actually tastes better than it sounds. Sometimes Mother made a very thin, brandy flavoured custard instead, and in either case, there was always a bowl of whipped cream to spoon on top. In America, we made the traditional hard sauce, and quite recently I have been given yet another recipe for plum pudding sauce. As with all the best Christmas recipes, this has a long history of family Christmases, and is well worth trying.

- 1 egg
- 1½ cups icing sugar
- 1 tablespoon cold water
- 3 tablespoons brandy

Separate the egg, and beat the yolk with the sugar and cold water for 12 minutes. Heat in the top of a double boiler, still beating, and when hot but not boiling, fold in the stiffly beaten egg white. Measure the brandy into your serving bowl, add the sauce to it and serve at once.

My Dutch friend, Sophie, says her childhood Christmases were graced with English plum pudding served with a thin, clear, apricot sauce. We've neither of us been able to find a recipe for this, although it is a mouth-watering memory. It is one of those things which might repay experimenting.

AND IN CONCLUSION

BUT SURELY THERE CAN BE NO
CONCLUSION. EVEN I, WHO HAVE SPENT
TIME AND THOUGHT GATHERING THIS
TOGETHER FOR YOU, FEEL THAT THERE
ARE STILL MANY THINGS I'VE LEFT
OUT. (THAT MARVELLOUS RECIPE OF MY
GRANDMOTHER'S FOR INSTANCE WHICH
BEGINS CHEERFULLY "TAKE ¼ LB.
BUTTER, LESS THAN ¼ LB. SUGAR AND
MORE THAN ¼ LB. FLOUR".) AND YOU,
FOR WHOM IT IS WRITTEN, CERTAINLY
KNOW IT IS INCOMPLETE.

If there is a lack of evenness in the recipes it is because, of course, they have been written by different people. I have included them, wherever possible, exactly as they were given to me and they therefore each carry with them something of the personality of the giver. This is the way I feel it should be. Yet it is still incomplete.

For, to this heritage which I pass on to you, must be added your own. The rum balls which for years have been Frances's contribution to the Christmas Cookie Tray. Kate's own special way of making pork chop casserole. And who knows what else as the years go by. Perhaps as was sometimes done, I should have left you a few blank pages marked "For Your Own Recipes", but somehow I've never quite approved of that system. You need space to work in, and freedom to elaborate and comment. Strength of mind, too, and honesty to choose and weed out where necessary. (My mother has written beside one of her recipes "This cake is dry. Don't make.") So, buy yourselves exercise books and write your own recipes in it as you go along. Write them with care and love and appreciation for the friendship and sharing they represent, and one day you'll find you've gathered a whole lifetime of memories between those covers.

♥♥♥♥♥♥♥♥♥♥♥♥♥♥♥♥♥♥♥♥♥♥♥♥♥♥♥♥♥♥

Once when I was a very small girl, I won a prize for an essay on "My Mother". One sentence of it has come down in family history.

I wrote "I love my mother. She spends most of her time in the kitchen". In all honesty and sincerity, I meant it as a compliment, though some people may not see it that way. And even I don't always find the thought of spending most of my time in the kitchen appealing. In my mother's case it certainly was not literally true, for she did a good many other things in her life besides cook, but I don't think I meant it to be taken literally. I was simply trying to express the pleasure of being in a kitchen where cooking was done with humour and love. I hope that you, also, have known this pleasure and will continue to know it. I hope that, like me, you (and maybe your children after you) can say with some pride – and a flood of memories – "My mother was a good cook, too".

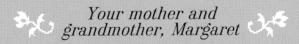

Your mother and grandmother, Margaret

♥♥♥♥♥♥♥♥♥♥♥♥♥♥♥♥♥♥♥♥♥♥♥♥♥♥♥♥♥

CONVERSION GUIDE*

LIQUID MEASURES

ML	FL OZ	VOLUME
5 ml		1 teaspoon
10 ml		1 dessertspoon
15/20 ml	½ fl oz	1 tablespoon
60 ml	2 fl oz	¼ cup
80 ml	2 ½ fl oz	⅓ cup
125 ml	4 fl oz	½ cup
150 ml	5 fl oz	¼ pint/1 gill
185 ml	6 fl oz	¾ cup
190 ml	6 ⅔ fl oz	⅓ pint/ 1 tea cup
250 ml	9 fl oz	1 cup
	10 fl oz	½ pint
375 ml	13 fl oz	1½ cups
500 ml	17 fl oz	2 cups
570 ml	20 fl oz	1 pint
750 ml	26 fl oz	3 cups
875 mls	30 fl oz	1½ pints
1 litre	35 fl oz	4 cups

WEIGHT MEASURES

G/KG	OZ	LB
25/30 g	1 oz	
40 g	1½ oz	
55 g	2 oz	
100 g	3½ oz	
115 g	4 oz	¼ lb
150 g	5½ oz	
200 g	7 oz	
225 g	8 oz	½ lb
250 g	9 oz	
300 g	10½ oz	
350 g	12 oz	
400 g	14 oz	
455 g	16 oz	1 lb
500 g	17½ oz	1 lb 2 oz
900	32 oz	2 lb
1 kg	35¼ oz	2 lb 4 oz

* This guide is an approximation only

OVEN TEMPERATURES

°C	°F	GAS	
100	200	½	
120	235	½	Cool/Slow
140	275	1	
160	315	2–3	
180	350	4	Moderate
200	400	6	
210	415	6–7	Hot/Quick

INDEX

Published in 2008 by Murdoch Books Pty Limited.
First published as *Mother Was a Good Cook, Too*, Jack Pollard, Sydney, 1974.

Murdoch Books Australia
Pier 8/9
23 Hickson Road
Millers Point NSW 2000
Phone: +61 (0) 2 8220 2000
Fax: +61 (0) 2 8220 2558
www.murdochbooks.com.au

Murdoch Books UK Limited
Erico House, 6th Floor
93–99 Upper Richmond Road
Putney, London SW15 2TG
Phone: +44 (0) 20 8785 5995
Fax: +44 (0) 20 8785 5985
www.murdochbooks.co.uk

Chief Executive: Juliet Rogers
Publishing Director: Kay Scarlett

Editor: Emma Hutchinson
Design Concept: Lauren Camilleri
Design: Lauren Camilleri and Joanna Byrne
Production: Monique Layt

National Library of Australia Cataloguing-in-Publication Data
    Dunn, Margaret.
        Mrs Harvey's sister-in-law and other tasty dishes.

        Includes index.
        ISBN 978 1 74196 080 8 (hbk.).

        1. Cookery. 2. Food - Social aspects. I. Title.

        641.5

A catalogue record for this book is available from the British Library.

Colour separation by Splitting Image Colour Studio, Melbourne, Australia

Printed by i-Book Printing Ltd. in 2007. PRINTED IN CHINA.

IMPORTANT: Those who might be at risk from the effects of salmonella
poisoning (the elderly, pregnant women, young children and those suffering
from immune deficiency diseases) should consult their doctor with any
concerns about eating raw eggs.